My Body, My Soul

One Woman's Journey to Reclaim Both

Vandee Crane

outskirts press

"To live is the rarest thing in the world.
Most people just exist. That is all."
- Oscar Wilde

Dedication I dedicate this book to every child who is abused or deprived of love. I dedicate this book to every boy, girl, and woman who is exploited in the trade of modern-day slavery. I dedicate this book to the individuals who work tireless hours to relieve the pain and devastation that is left as a result of these abuses. I dedicate this book to everyone who has loved and believed in me along the way. I dedicate this book to my offenders, without whose offenses, my story would not exist. Above all I dedicate this book to my Mother, who recently who made her Journey Home in March of 2014 and will never get the chance to read these words. Without her I would not exist... And I would like to give very special thanks to Dr. & Mrs. Joe Armstrong. Through the integrity of their Christian values, I was for the first time in my life able to experience what it is like to be a part of a loving family and live in a safe place where many of my childhood dreams became a reality, the place in which this book was authored.

Intention In a world in which we are all experts on everything except for ourselves, I offer to you my story, and the innate expertise that comes along with it. I am not claiming to be an expert on child psychology, on the epidemic of human trafficking, or on addictions, but rather an expert on what it will take to heal the deepest wounds that exist in the psyche. Above all, I consider myself to be an expert on myself and how I as an Indigenous Woman have had to learn to heal in a world full of colonial violence. With that, I offer to you my experience with the intent of educating you; opening your eyes, your mind, and your heart, and giving you some insight into your own life, your own suffering, and your own healing. Above all I offer to you my story with the intention to make you feel, to feel right down to very core of your existence, so that you will experience your own humanity, giving you full permission to tell your own story of strength, survival and above all H.O.P.E (hearing other people's experience).

Table of Contents

Preface

There were times that I thought that maybe this story was not meant to be told. That it would not be of interest to others for it lacked intrinsic value. Aside from my internal self-doubt, there were the external challenges that I faced in writing this book as well. You see this will be my third attempt to record my story. The other two attempts were lost due to technical issues and my failure to keep consistent and reliable backups of my data. In a conversation with another individual, after recounting all the misfortune in the process of writing my personal memoirs, the individual replied, "It sounds like that book isn't supposed to be written." I instantly had a knee-jerk reaction, and responded with a firm declaration, "That's not it! It just wasn't supposed to be written through the lens in which I was viewing myself, my life, my story, and the world in general."

After the last loss of data, which occurred on April 28, 2014 (exactly one month after the death of my Mother), I could feel myself being pulled into the downward spiral of devastation, grief and loss, and self-pity. My frustration and loss of hope grew with every attempt to find the data, every thought that maybe the backup was just simply hiding in a place that I hadn't checked yet. I could feel the depression and despair setting in. I could see signs of my developing emotional crisis showing in my home: the dishes that were undone in the sink, the piles of laundry that I just couldn't bring myself to fold and put away, my daily "to-do lists" that were going undone, most of all that awful feeling of the heaviness of anxiety creeping into my heart. The night of Thursday May 1, *I made the decision* that I was not going to allow self-doubt to get the best of me, that I hadn't survived this much to accept defeat now. I set the intention that all that I desired to grow in my life, I would nourish with love, and that all the feelings I had been feeling were in no way loving, as there was no joy to be found in those thoughts or emotions. I am a strong believer that our thoughts are our conversation with the Creator and with the Universe at large, and once we make a decision and set an intention, Creator, the entire Universe, everything and everyone around us begins to conspire in ways to support us in that intention. We just have to be the ones to initiate that first step, making the decision.

Not surprisingly, I was provided with just what I needed to be re-inspired. On Saturday, May 3, 2014, I received an unexpected but greatly welcomed phone call from a woman who I had worked with in Santa Fe named Kari Meredith. I would be honored to have the right to call her a friend, but up until now, I believe our relationship could most correctly be described as an acquaintance or a business associate. Nevertheless, I do believe that this phone call was the beginning of a beautiful friendship, for she provided me with exactly what I needed at that moment in time. Initially she was just calling to confirm a speaking date for an upcoming event here in New Mexico. Our conversation focused, then moved on to the topic of following your dreams and she shared with me how she had recently left her job in order to follow hers and how she too was in the process of writing her first book. Kari was able to give me a lot of practical advice, which is always appreciated, but the gift that she gave me that day was the gift of believing in me. The words she used to describe what I had to offer and how my gift would be so unique and valuable to the world uplifted me from any residual ill feeling I was holding onto. Then she finished with saying, "This book is the key, Vandee ...this book is the key to all of your other dreams coming true." In that moment, I knew that she was correct. I have had the dream in my heart of writing a book that would change the world since I first started college at age sixteen. For so many years, I listened to my ego, which told me things like, "psshh, who are you to write a book? To change the world? What a laugh!" As it turns out, writing this book is a part of the Blueprint of my Soul. If it wasn't meant to be, why would Creator have placed it in my heart? As if my thoughts had been heard, I received even more confirmation on that fateful day.

I had just returned from my afternoon walk and decided to go back to the main house on the ranch. As I walked in, Dr. Armstrong announced that I was just in time for the races, that they were lining up at the gates. I had no idea that that Saturday was the day of the Kentucky Derby, as I hadn't made a point to watch the Kentucky Derby since childhood. I sat down to watch the race. Mrs. Armstrong explained to me that the owner of the horse named Uncle Sigh had pledged to donate all the winnings to the Wounded Warrior Foundation. Coming from a family full of combat veterans, I of course decided that that was the horse I was rooting for and that horse was actually in the lead for the first half of the race. Soon another horse gained the lead and took the race. I was disappointed, but I soon was reminded that nothing happens by accident. The announcer began to tell the story of the winning horse, California Chrome, a true story of an unanticipated champion. You see, California Chrome was going to be the owners' first horse as they decided to enter into the world of horse racing. One of the owners, Coburn, had a dream that this chestnut colt was going to win the Kentucky Derby before the colt was foaled. He was scoffed at by horse racing cohorts in thinking that this was going to be a winner, since the colt wasn't coming from a lineage of champion race horses. In fact, he was called a "dumbass" by those same cohorts in the racing community for even announcing that declaration. In good humor, he and his partner named their racing team "Dumbass Partners," DAP for short. All of this transpired in 2011. On May 3, 2014, California Chrome won the $2 million Kentucky Derby, which just also happened to be Coburn's 61st birthday. I was holding back the tears as my heart began to overflow with joy, hope, and gratitude, for I knew that just as his had, my dreams would also come true. I was convinced that the writing of my book would commence, with a fervor and passion that had been missing before. It was time! But as though I needed more confirmation, I received another message loud and clear. Later that evening,

I logged onto my Facebook account only to see a picture of my dear beautiful friend Jessica Rose in a polka dot sun dress and a swanky sun hat to match. She had attended the Kentucky Derby that day, a dream that she had had since childhood. Some may say that this was all co-incidence or that maybe I was just looking for deeper meaning in that which was really mundane, but it does not matter how it is perceived by anyone but me, for it was the answer to my personal doubts, the confirmation and the permission that I needed to move forward.

Rather than viewing the task of re-writing a book that was close to being completed as a daunting and inconvenient rite of passage, I made the choice to view this opportunity as a gift, a gift to re-write my story from another perspective. As I mentioned, my Mother had passed away on March 28, 2014, leaving me as the matriarch in my family at the age of thirty-one years old. There was a shift in me, in the lens through which I viewed the world. There was so much healing that came as result of my Mother dying, that it must in fact be the correct lens through which this story is to be told.

Part 1

A Life Against Me

1

A Story Unlike Any Other

"A book must be an ice-axe to break the
seas frozen inside the Soul."
- Frank Kafka

MY NAME IS Vandee Crane and I am a grateful recovering addict. I am also a Counselor, a Wellness Coach, a Speaker, a Yoga Teacher, a Writer, and child sexual exploitation and trafficking (CSET) Survivor Leader. But above all those things I am a Woman of great Faith and an Wazazi Woman. My previous attempts to write this story were frustrating to say the least. I was trying to write my story from the perspective of a "professional author", constantly editing, critiquing, reading and re-reading my work. "No, this isn't right," I would think to myself. "This event must be explained before this event can be understood, and this isn't in chronological order so I need to go back and figure out exactly where I need to plug this event in." Then it dawned on me one day, my life has been *anything* but linear and static, so why am I trying to tell my story in a linear and static fashion? This realization resulted in my letting go of a lot of that frustration.

In order to be authentic in my writing, I was going to need to let go of that attachment to perfectionism that still lingered in my life.

Shortly after that realization, I was on a trip to Northern New Mexico to show a couple of my new German friends around, see the sites, and eat amazing New Mexican food. While I was there I had stopped to pick up the local free publication, *The Santa Fe Reporter*, to see what events might be going on, to read Rob Brezney's horoscope column, etc. While browsing through the events for the current week, I happened across a writer's workshop that just happened be on the same day that I would be speaking at a professional training near Santa Fe in the very near future. The workshop was being presented by a best-selling author named of Tom Bird. To be honest, I had never heard of Tom Bird before, nor had I ever heard of any of his books. It was the title of the workshop that caught my interest. The workshop was titled *How to Write Your Best-Seller in a Weekend and Get it Published.* I would like to consider myself somewhat of an empiricist, in the sense that I rarely buy into something unless I have an experience of it, but unlike your typical scientific empiricist, my experiences don't necessarily need to be tangible or observable and measurable. These experiences can also come to me through intuition and dreams. At any rate, I didn't necessarily believe the part about writing a best-seller in a weekend, as I was always taught that "haste makes waste," but the part about getting your book published was what really struck my interest, especially since I did not have the slightest idea how to get published, or even really whom to talk to. So, I called to register. The ad had mentioned that the first ten people to register would be free for the workshop, and at that moment, "free" was one of my favorite words, as money was pretty tight, so I called to inquire and potentially register. The receptionist at Body, a local yoga studio, boutique, and restaurant, informed me that I was the first person to call for registration, so I reserved my free spot.

When things work out that effortlessly, I believe that it's meant to be, as if another puzzle piece of Creator's Divine Blueprint is being revealed. If I am struggling to make things happen, I take that as an indicator that it is my will and not that of the Divine.

Fast-forwarding a couple of weeks to March 20, 2014, I showed up at the Yoga studio/boutique/restaurant for the workshop and boy, did I ever feel out of place! As I walked into the room with my cowboy boots clicking, it was as if all conversations stopped and everyone paused their conversation to turn their attention to me, in my whole young, wild and free, heavily tattooed glory. I walked into a conference room of highbrow, all Caucasian, over- fifty crowd. As I often do, I said to myself, "What did I just get myself into? " But I took a deep breath, checked my posture, and walked into the room to find a seat. I attempted to make eye contact with a couple of people and smile, hoping to engage a conversation, but had no such luck. Most refused to even return the smile. If this was the audience that reads this author's books, I thought that I might not connect with the author either. But something inside me told me to stay.

A short while later, a handsome man who had been mingling up at the front of the room stood up and introduced himself as Tom Bird, the best-selling author. He opened the workshop by qualifying himself. Maybe it's just me, but I have a hard time listening to others go on about their achievements. Up until a couple of years ago, I had always thought that this was because to me, that indicated that the person was full of themselves. I now recognize that that reaction has less to do with them and more to do with me. A few years back, while taking a course in Positive Psychology, the class was asked to stand up in front of the room and talk about all the ways in which they wanted to improve themselves, essentially what they didn't like about themselves. After we all took a turn standing before the class and talking about our defects, we were then asked to come back up in front of the class once more and talk about the things that we loved about ourselves, our accomplishments, and all the things that we completely accepted. I have a feeling that if this exercise were being done at an Ivy League university, or in any college that hosted students of a higher socioeconomic class, the experience would have turned out a lot differently. But this was no Ivy League university. This was a four-year college in a small community in Northern New Mexico called Española.

The majority of students, including myself were either of Hispanic or Native descent, and I could guarantee that we all grew up in families that struggled and endured hardship that only individuals from lower socioeconomic groups would know. This has an incredible effect on the intrinsic value of oneself. There is a constant ongoing dialogue of not being good enough, so of course, all of the students found it much easier to discuss the things that they didn't like about themselves, than the things they did like. In fact, sadly, some women weren't even able to identify things that they loved about themselves. Although this can be partially attributed to cultural relativity, a lot of it was just lacking a positive self-image, something that I have struggled with a majority of my own life. So, I gently reminded myself of this so that I could drop the wall that I was beginning to build when I started to judge the author based on his introduction.

Have you ever been at a workshop, in church, at a class, in a Twelve Step meeting or any other type of public forum and you heard the message of the speaker so crystal clearly that it felt like it was intended specifically for you, even though you were in a room full of other people? This was one of those specific occasions for me. The author, Tom Bird, started talking about his personal experience that led him to write his own book, and his internal process sounded familiar, eerily familiar in fact. What he said next came as such a relief to me. He told us to throw out everything that we learned in academia about writing, at least if we wanted to write a best-seller. He went on to explain that people don't buy books because of your knowledge, that you could in fact know everything in the world about a particular topic, but that isn't what makes a best-seller. He continued by explaining that writing was a spiritual act, the act of allowing the Divine to flow through you. The real reason that a majority of people read books is to feel, to access their own humanity. And, that if you had the ability to make people feel through your writing, then you in fact had a best seller.

This was another one of those Divine synchronicities that caused a light bulb to go off in my head, a road marker, if you will, signaling to me that I was going in the right direction. As I had mentioned, I had a speaking engagement earlier that day at the SuperHealth International Professional Training. I was honored to tell my story in front of a group of individuals not only from all over the country, but from all over the world, from all different walks and professions of life; however, there was one thing that we did have in common and that was that we all practiced Kundalini Yoga, and in one way or another the practice had deeply impacted our lives. Kundalini Yoga is one of the more challenging forms of Yoga, but it is also said that it is a Yoga that anyone could benefit from, even someone who has paralysis. Kundalini Yoga is also referred to as the Yoga of Awareness. "It is a dynamic, powerful tool designed to give you the experience of your own soul."

Whenever and wherever I speak, I make a point to say a prayer before I begin. I pray that I may just get out of the way and allow the Divine to flow through me so that I may say exactly what needs to be said in order to reach the audience members and deliver to them the message that they need to hear. So far, this has worked out very well as the audiences have laughed, cried, gasped, shaken, and nodded their heads and come up to me at the end of every engagement sharing their profound experience. So, it dawned on me…I already have the best-selling story; I just needed to capture it in a way that was authentic and not contrived. Hearing that writing a best-seller was a spiritual act made it so much more accessible to me. After that day, I felt as though more details to my own Divine Blueprint had been revealed. I was ready to move forward with renewed ambition and clearer vision.

Now that I have disclosed to you that this story will unfold in a cyclic and spiritual manner, rather than linear and secular, I should also let you know that since childhood, I have always been drawn to the mystic side of life. I grew up Catholic; however, my Grandmother always wanted me to stay connected to our Traditional Native beliefs. She embraced international travel and the customs of many different cultures. I can only hope that that richness that she left with me shows through in my writing as it has certainly been a huge influence on my perception and life experiences. It has added so much more meaning to life than just experiencing life as a collective series of mundane events. I have always felt that Great Spirit has always had a strong presence in my life, all the way back to when I had my conversations with Creator in telephone booths as a young child. I really don't remember that infatuation as a child, but I often heard stories and in the photos that I have I really did look deep in thought for a three- or four-year-old. After all, there is an entire world that exists outside the limits of human vision and hearing. It seems to me that children, and even more so animals, are more in tune with this world than the majority of adults. It always saddens my heart to witness an adult discount a child's experience of miracles and magic. I do, however, remember being very much in tune with that world. I was blessed to have a Mother and Grandmother who not only did not discredit these experiences but taught me to embrace them. There was a time in my life that I became cynical myself and laughed at those who expressed interest in the metaphysical, but luckily I was able to resuscitate that part of my own psyche. As a result, much of this story will be told from the perspective of the Sacred feminine. My spiritual experiences are so deeply interwoven into my story, there is no way for me to tell it any other way.

Lastly, I will mention this...there are parts of my story that are so humanly inconceivable that it feels like I am watching a horror movie when these images flashback into my mind. How could I have survived these experiences? How is my mind still as intact as it is? I feel so far removed from this life that I once lived that it almost feels like somebody else's story. But it is my story, that shaped who I am today, and for that I am infinitely grateful.

2

Growing Up At-Risk

"Truth is stranger than fiction, but it is because Fiction is obliged to stick to possibilities; Truth isn't."
- Mark Twain

IN JUNE OF 2013, although I was intent on focusing on the non-profit I had founded and relying on independent contracting to pay the bills in the meantime, I found myself called to looking at the employment section of the Craigslist website. I saw an ad posted for several program director positions at a local organization that offered services to at-risk youth in Santa Fe, New Mexico. Although I had heard several nightmarish stories from other colleagues who had previously worked there as case managers, the positions that were posted were for program directors. Intuitively, I felt called to apply for these positions, even though I had other intentions at the time. Having heard these awful stories about the agency, one such person calling it "Satan's Pit," I figured with an upper management position such as the ones that were posted, I would be able to affect change for the positive within said agency. And whenever I feel intuitively drawn to something, it usually ends up that Creator had a purpose for me being there.

After going through the interview process, I was hired, and started the position in early July, just as I was finishing up another contract. I was mortified by the condition of the program for which I had just taken responsibility. The property and buildings were nice but had been poorly maintained. There was no structure to the program, and it seemed as if the program was still running from a previous paradigm that would have been acceptable in the early 1990s. There was a general malaise among staff and clients. It was discouraging to say the least. But I believe that the most horrifying part was the culture of this agency that seemed to work against the at- risk youth they were intending to serve, keeping them disenfranchised and denying them the essential skills that are needed to recover from trauma to lead healthy and responsible lives. These findings of mine were further reinforced by the fact that a client committed suicide in the program on my fourth day of work. What this agency was doing was obviously not working and the clients were dying as a result of their negligence and the culture of degradation and psychological abuse that had become normalized within the agency's culture. However, after filing reports with the Licensing and Regulations Board and they found no issues with their practices, I realized the issue was more systemic and deeply rooted in the professional community than I had first though.

Having come from a program that received best practices and standards for the recovery work done with human trafficking victims, I found it most imperative to start with educating and empowering the youth so that they could protect themselves from exploitation, because as vulnerable as they were, they were prime targets for such crimes. I was actually rather surprised that this agency had no apparent involvement with the anti-human trafficking initiatives that had become so prevalent in Santa Fe in the previous couple of years. I was extremely ambitious in my goal of not only educating and empowering clients, but also of bringing the staff up to par with the most current trauma-informed skills and tools available in the field. Unfortunately, this ambition drew a lot of negative attention from my supervisor, who we will call Jane Hoffner. Not only was she vehemently opposed to my goals; she was vehemently opposed to me in general as a person and displayed an overall bitterness and general dislike of clients and staff alike. I often wonder how people like this find their way into careers in the mental health field, being as unstable as they are themselves. It is not like the career pays a lot of money. You have to get fulfillment out of helping others and she made it very apparent that she was *not* that type of person. It was as though she wanted the at-risk youth to stay at-risk, and I had a gut feeling why. I had heard about the billionaire child sex trafficker that had a location outside of Santa Fe named Zorro Ranch. I heard about the years' worth of coverups and all the noteworthy politicians who attend his parties, but I had no concrete evidence that the two were connected. All I knew was that I had an awful feeling in the pit of my stomach, and that I had been led to this agency for a reason. Occasionally over the years I would call the FBI Tip Line to report my suspicions and felt I was only being gaslit or discredited in the call screening. Seven years later the truth of Jeffrey Epstein and his pedophile playgrounds have surfaced; however, they are still making little to no mention of the investigations in New Mexico.

In order to begin to understand the crime of human trafficking, specifically child sex trafficking, I feel that it is necessary that we begin with the most common factor that leaves a person vulnerable to this crime: being "at-risk." First, we will examine from a general standpoint what it means to be "at-risk." We will make our way from general to specific and within these specifics I will share with you the intimate details of what it meant for me as a child growing up at-risk.

"At-risk"...a term that we have all heard, but what does it really mean? Google will provide you with a plethora of definitions, criteria, prevention programs, signs and symptoms, etc. But what is the deeper meaning when we move past the ways to intellectualize it? I believe that the notion of being "at-risk" begins far before a child is born. I believe that it rests in the DNA of that family, not just in the genetic sense, but in the epigenetic sense. Generational trauma is something that is very present in our world, but I don't believe that it is something that is well understood, and it's definitely not something that is taken into consideration by world leaders, lawmakers, or the population in general. More and more scientific evidence is pointing to epigenetic theory as more than just a theory. Basically, the notion is that whatever happened in the lives of our ancestors, whether it was a life filled with trauma or a life filled with treasures, the emotional response that they had to the events in their lives affected their DNA and in turn still affects ours, leading to the same patterns being recreated over and over again, generation after generation.

So where shall I begin my at-risk story? I suppose the place in history that would make the most sense for you as the reader would be with my Mother's background. My Mother was the middle child in a middle-class Catholic family. Both of her parents, my maternal Grandmother and Grandfather were combat veterans. My Dutch-Irish Grandfather served in WWII & the "forgotten war," officially known as the Korean War, and my Grandmother served as a nurse in the Army during World War II, stationed mainly in France and Spain. In retrospect, I can honestly say that my maternal Grandparents both met the criteria for having severe, chronic Post Traumatic Stress Disorder (PTSD), but of course back then, that was not a diagnosis. I believe the popular term was "shell-shocked," but even that term carried with it the stigma of weakness, of not being able to handle what was seen and experienced in combat, so they never addressed the trauma they had experienced during their involvement in the war. Veterans just returned to "business as usual" when they came back home. And "business as usual" in the era of the 1940s and 50s meant finding a spouse, getting a house, having children, and living "happily ever after" as a nuclear family. I think that when we look back at those times as a culture we can verifiably say that that approach of returning to "business as usual" is not only detrimental for the veteran that is returning from war, but also extremely unhealthy for the entire family. One cannot turn on the news today without hearing talk of the current rates of PTSD among vets returning from the wars in the Middle East, the associated suicides, domestic violence, and even mass shootings that have been correlated with unresolved symptoms of severe PTSD. So the first risk that I would like to highlight is the genetic predisposition for PTSD.

I can speak from personal experience regarding living with PTSD. In my experience there are two ways you can live with it. The first is to go on with "business as usual," ignoring the symptoms and acting as if there is nothing out of balance. The second way to live with PTSD is recognizing that there is in fact a disharmonious state that you are dealing with internally, learning about what symptoms you are experiencing, and taking proactive steps to manage the symptoms. I have lived both ways. The latter is much preferable, unless you prefer to suffer. The former method of dealing with the PTSD, or should I say the method of denying that you have symptoms associated with living through a traumatic experience, is very similar to having an infected wound. You can't totally deny it's there, but you are not completely willing to look at the severity of it. You cover it up with a Band-Aid, so you don't have to deal with what lies beneath the surface. In real life this metaphorical Band-Aid might be drugs and/or alcohol to numb the emotional pain. The Band-Aid may also come in the form of overeating, gambling, preoccupation with sex, pornography, or excessive shopping...basically anything that allows us that momentary escape from the emotional suffering. But you see, it is that and *only* that: momentary escape. The wound is still there and it's not healing. And much like an infected wound, trauma only gets worse as the symptoms go unaddressed. When we have an infected wound, it begins to fester and without the necessary intervention will eventually result in gangrene and lead to an amputation or possibly death due to the infection becoming systemic. Post Traumatic Stress Disorder is no different. The more we choose to ignore the symptoms, the more pervasive and systemic the maladaptive thinking and behavior becomes, until it is accepted as the baseline. What was once severely dysfunctional becomes the norm for the individual and possibly even the family. When it becomes the norm for the family, the trauma along with the maladaptive behaviors are passed down from generation to generation. That is the core definition of generational trauma. My family was no exception.

My Grandparents returned from the war, they met, fell in love, and had children, all before dealing with the demons that they brought back with them from being at war. I don't know when it began or if there was a definitive starting point, as these accounts are from vague descriptions from my Grandmother, but at some point my Grandfather became a raging alcoholic and began to beat my Grandmother and abuse the children. My Grandmother recalled how she left one time, packed up the three children in her Studebaker and drove cross-country from California to Washington, DC in the mid to late fifties. Women driving across country to get away from an abusive spouse was rare in that era, so I know things must have been unbearable. Rather than deal with his demons from WWII, my grandfather went off to war again and served in the Korean War. I am not sure for how long, but my Grandmother resided with her Mother and three children until my Grandfather returned from combat once again and had "his act cleaned up." This apparently meant that he had renounced hard liquor and committed to no longer beating his wife and children. They eventually moved back in together and moved the family to Florida. The abuse never ended; it just became more covert.

From the outside, the family appeared to have it together. My Grandfather worked as a parts manager, my Grandmother was a rather successful artist that was very involved in the community, and their children all attended an affluent Catholic school. Looking back in photo albums there were good times: family get-togethers, family vacations, and extracurricular activities (football, marching band, basketball, etc.). Everyone's needs appeared to be met, at least from the outside. My Mother appeared to be the princess of the family, being the only girl. Although the family appeared to have everything together from the outside, there was a far different story that was being told from inside those walls.

My Mother had me at twenty-nine years old. She had never lived independently from her parents. Yes, she worked jobs here and there and had lived at the family's second home that we owned on the same street, but she had never truly left the nest. She conceived me out of wedlock, which today isn't thought about twice, but at that time, in a Catholic family, was still very frowned upon. Although my Mother never directly communicated this with me, I imagine that shame, regret, and self-loathing were the core emotions that consumed her during the pregnancy, the reasons for which I will disclose in a later chapter.

I came into this world at 4:19 pm Eastern Standard Time on June 7, 1982, born at Orlando Regional Medical Center. I can always remember the time as my Mother made it a point to explain that I "chose" to be born during the season finale of Star Trek. It was a difficult birth, the labor lasting for some 15 to 20 hours, so I was told. I was born in a full breech position and the delivery was traumatizing to say the least. One would assume this to be traumatizing for the Mother, but in other medical theories, such as Chinese medicine, the etiology and pathogenesis for an organism are traced back to any trauma or shock that occurred during the pregnancy or birth. In the Chinese medical theory, trauma and shock are profoundly important physiological events in diagnosis and treatment as these types of events have a huge influence on the circulation of blood and energy in the body and directly affect the physiological and emotional functioning of the heart. This became very apparent to me after my first experience receiving an acupuncture treatment in my early twenties. The young doctor of Chinese Medicine had gently placed a needle into a point corresponding to the heart in the center of my chest. I felt an electrical surge through my body that resulted in my nearly jumping off the table with a loud gasp. The young woman looked at me compassionately and said, "You have a lot of heart troubles, don't you?" My response was, "no, not to my knowledge, but heart disease does run in the family." She then explained that it had more to do with the emotional heart, but that if the issues go unaddressed they can lead to physical issues with the heart. There was a clue, *unaddressed emotional heart issues.* She left the room to allow me to relax during the treatment. The tears began to silently flow.

I don't recall much of my early childhood. I was told I was spoiled, which I don't doubt, being an only child. I look at pictures and in the beginning I saw a very bright, happy, little girl who was full of light and love. But as my age progressed in the childhood photos the emotional suffering, lack of confidence, and self-loathing began to show outwardly.

Shortly after I had quit drinking in my mid-twenties, I began to have "flashbacks," which are a typical symptoms of PTSD. One of these initial flashbacks was of my early childhood. I must have been somewhere around the age of two, as I know that I was potty-trained. I recall standing at the screen door of my family's home watching my Mother pull out of the driveway in her yellow Ford Pinto. I was having a tantrum, typical of most any two-year-old whose Mother is leaving them for possibly the first time to return to school, but the emotions that I felt were what I found the most disturbing. I remember feeling unsafe, abandoned, unprotected, and fearful. I was screaming and clawing at the screen door like an animal. This fear shortly turned to rage as my Grandmother led me away from the door. I remember feeling an immense frustration that I had not the words to explain these intense emotions that I was feeling, so I consciously made the decision to defecate in my pants. I knew I had been potty-trained previous to this episode, as I remembered my Grandmother's response: "Shame on you! You know better than that! Why didn't you tell me you had to go to the bathroom?" I wanted to tell her so much more, but I just didn't have the words to communicate those intense, all-consuming emotions.

The interesting thing about memories, as we have discovered from studying the brain, is that painful memories create the deepest grooves. They are the memories that are the most easily recalled. The other major interesting discovery about the way memories work is that each time we recall an event, we are not actually remembering the event itself. We are actually remembering the last time we remembered it. So what exactly does that mean in terms of our cognition? Simply that every time we recall a memory, we have the opportunity to rewrite the story. Not the actual facts of the story, but the subjective part of the story, the way in which we perceive it. That said, when I experience these flashbacks and onslaughts of sad memories, I make it a point to remember these facts and incorporate coping skills, so as not to get caught in the drama of the details. Just because I have blocked out most of my childhood does not mean that there were not happy times amidst the turmoil and trauma.

Following the memory of being that frightened and enraged two-year-old, comes my next memory, which incorporates my first conscious encounter of having a mind and mood altering experience. I must have been in preschool or somewhere there about. Like many small children of that era (because we did not have handheld electronics) I was obsessed with pressing elevator buttons and pumping gas. Now that I think about it, I was obsessed with any action that allowed me to feel like I had some element of control. On one occasion when my Mother had stopped to put gas in the car, I was standing next to the pump, "assisting," and my Mother had walked around the other side of the car for a moment. When she came back around, she found me with my nose near the pump inhaling the fumes. Of course, I had no clue what I was doing; I just knew that it made me feel good, that I no longer felt the burden of emotional pain, at least in that moment. She scolded me and educated me on the fact that fumes from gasoline were harmful, but nevertheless, that experience of escapism stuck with me.

There were other common themes in my childhood that I now know to be early signs of an addict/alcoholic and the symptoms of a child who had been sexually abused. I never felt like I fit in, most likely because I didn't. I was "overly sensitive," overweight, out of shape. I wet my bed regularly until I was twelve, I was chronically ill with ear infections, tonsillitis, sinus infections, etc. I hated going to school because I was such a social misfit, it became remarkably unbearable, so I learned to exaggerate my symptoms in order to skip school. I enjoyed being at home more than anything else, at least during the day. The adults were busy with their responsibilities and I was left alone to read encyclopedias, sort through and memorize my Animal Planet cards, look through *National Geographic* magazines, and spend time with our household pets. There were no social pressures, I did not experience the pain of rejection, and I got to satisfy my quest for knowledge, but this did not occur as often or for as long as I would have liked. I always had to go back to that horrible social experiment known as Catholic School.

I did, however, always enjoy going to Mass, but that came to an abrupt end when my hands began to sweat profusely, around the age of eight. I still enjoyed Mass, but every time we approached the time where we would hold hands to say the Lord's Prayer, it became a social nightmare, much like the rest of my childhood. Eventually, my mind was always preoccupied with how I could hide my sweaty hands or slip out of church and hide in the bathroom to escape it.

The most prominent part of my childhood was my emotional out-bursts. I remember being able to contain my emotions through the day for the most part, but at home was a different story. Crying myself to sleep was a common theme, more often than not. It was as though all of the negativity in the home was being directly channeled through me. As I had mentioned, my Grandfather's methods of abuse were still alive and well, just more covert. There were more often than not argu-ments, yelling, crying, screaming, insults, etc. The crying and scream-ing were for the most part my reaction to the general negative air in the home. To clarify, my Mother and I resided with my Grandparents in a three-bedroom, one-bath home in Central Florida. From as early as five or six years of age, I can clearly remember the sentiment of not wanting to be alive and being obsessed with my own death. I would imagine different ways that I knew people could die, such as drown-ing or being hit by a car, and I followed those thoughts by wonder-ing if anyone would care or even notice. When I didn't hate myself, I was preoccupied with the thought of being invisible or just not good enough. People were so unbearably cruel to each other and to me. I could not understand why people couldn't love and be genuinely kind to each other, even at such a young age. The prominent theme was always emotional suffering and emptiness. That void was always there for as long as I can remember.

Recalling the moment at the gas pump, I knew that I liked the smell of gasoline. However, that experience was secondary to what I felt inside: relief. And with this relief came the burst of what I now know to be dopamine in the brain, the neurotransmitter associated with the relief of suffering. At that moment, an addict was born. I had finally discovered a way to numb the pain of not receiving the love that I so deeply desired. Throughout my childhood, I would continue this behavior, generally sneaking inhales from air-freshener aerosol spray cans when I felt an overwhelming sense of emotional suffering. Little did I know at that time that this behavior was the product of my repressing the experience of being sexually molested and anything that triggered the trauma related to growing up in a dysfunctional and abusive home.

Another form of emotional suffering that I distinctly recall was recurring nightmares. At a young age, I was exposed to horror movies such as "The Exorcist" and "The Amityville Horror." My Grandmother, although the sweetest, most enduring woman I have ever known, had a preoccupation with such things. I would stay up late with her and watch horror movies. It was my favorite thing to do on the weekends. Although my psyche was being filled with fuel for nightmares, it was a time for bonding and a time that I was protected from the sexual abuse that often occurred in the night. At some point I watched the Stephen King movie "IT." I already had a substantiated fear of clowns, but that didn't stop me from watching it. That movie spawned serious phobias that on some level, I still deal with today. It definitely planted seeds in my mind for this specific nightmare. I had this nightmare regularly for at least a couple of years. In the dream, I would be sleeping in my bedroom that I shared with my Mother, only to be awakened suddenly by the noisy arrival of the clown, Pennywise, from the movie "IT." I could hear as he entered my family's home with his distinct voice. I could hear the screams of my family members as they were being butchered in the living room. In my dream, Pennywise had a peg- leg. Once the sounds of my family being murdered ceased, I would then hear Pennywise thumping down the hall with that peg-leg, yelling, "I'm coming for you. There is no one left to save you now." And I would always wake up in terror, crying, having wet the bed. Not knowing that all of these symptoms were signs of a severely emotionally disturbed child who was being abused, I internalized these factors as merely things that were inherently wrong with me. It was just further evidence that I was defective, more evidence that I didn't belong in life.

From the age of two or three, I had a very "cute" habit of stealing my Mother's beer and taking a few gulps. I don't think I actually noticed the effect of alcohol until I was nine years old. On the weekends my Mother and I would head out to the New Smyrna area, along the east coast of Florida, to spend time with my Mother's best friend, Katherine, and Katherine's husband Lance. Katherine and Lance had a daughter that was a few years older than I, named Mandy. She was much like a cousin to me, as we had been visiting them for as long as I can remember. I rode my first horse at their farm when I was two years old. My very first addiction, even more than being under the influence of substances, was riding horses. I still remember that first ride. Apparently, my Mom did not know that Lance was going to put me up on their family horse, Rosie, a giant thoroughbred. He gently placed me in front of Mandy. Mandy and I proceeded to ride Rosie around in front of the house. I remember this being the most exhilarating experience, even at such a young age. I knew that this was going to be my passion. My Mother emerged from the house, shocked and a little hysterical. I was having a blast, waving and shouting, "Mommy! Mommy! Look at me!" Seeing that I was safe and having fun, she quickly calmed down and ran for her camera. I've mentioned that that was my first time riding, but never really allowed myself to enjoy the emotions attached to that memory until now, as tears of joy run down my cheeks.

I was introduced to a lot of things during my weekends up there. By the time I was nine, Mandy was sneaking beer and liquor from her parents and sneaking out to meet up with boyfriends. I was the awkward tagalong, the alibi. This was when I started noticing the effects of alcohol, that warm, numbing sensation that made you just not care. I enjoyed that altered reality where I didn't have to care that I was over-weight, or ugly, or socially awkward. It was a welcomed state to not feel so emotionally disturbed and out of place on this planet. Little did I know that I was just further compounding my emotional dysfunction. After all, we were just kids having fun...or so I thought.

It was at this age that another major event took place that would change the dynamics of my life, my Mother's life, and the dynamic of the entire family. As I mentioned previously, my Mother was a single parent and that meant working at the job that provided the most hours and paid the highest hourly wage that she could find for her experience and skill set. My Mother had never finished college. She had followed several different areas of study that she was interested in, such as landscape design, photography, journalism, and dental assisting, but never quite finished her coursework to earn a degree. She had various jobs throughout my childhood. At her last full-time job, she worked for a horticulture company. I'm not quite sure what her actual title was, but I called her a "plant lady" because she worked with plants. At this job she was required to go around to the different major hotels and theme parks that had accounts with the company and care for their plants. Part of the job required that she use her personal vehicle to haul around a 55-gallon drum on wheels that contained some sort of liquid to spray on the plants. After a couple of months or so of working at this job, she started to get ill, but doctors could never identify a specific cause for her general cluster of symptoms. She was eventually diagnosed with chronic fatigue syndrome and fibromyalgia. Not a whole lot was known about these conditions back then, as these diagnoses were only emerging at the time. As a child I couldn't under-stand why she just couldn't get better. She began sleeping all the time and her disposition greatly changed; she basically dropped out of her own life and in turn dropped out of mine. There was one such occa-sion when I remember feeling specifically crushed. I was ten years old and had been practicing and practicing to compete in the junior barrel racing event at the Volusia County Rodeo. She had not been feeling well, as by then she was always sick, but she had promised to meet us at the rodeo. When it came time for my debut, I was so incredibly nervous. I looked over to scan for my Mother and she was not there. I felt crushed. I realize now one of the most important needs for our psyche is to be seen and validated. Just as my Mother's life had become non-existent, I felt non-existent.

Growing up in a secretive, dysfunctional Catholic family there was a lot of shame. Nothing was out in the open. This is detrimental for obvious reasons as the abuse was never addressed, but there were obscured effects as well. One of these effects was the lack of good direction through positive education. The only education I recall around keeping myself safe was the common "do not talk to strangers," the very prudent version of "where babies come from," and the talk about "the treasure zone" and how no one should touch you there. I don't think any of this education was concrete, included practical terminology, or realistic consequences. Everything was taboo.

As a result of this familial and societal culture of shame, I felt shame for having questions about things that were only natural to question as a child at this age. For instance, my cousin introduced me to the book *The Joy of Sex*. My goodness, there were images in there that I could have never thought of! Imagine my confusion at seeing these images before having had a proper sex education talk.

Shortly after that, while riding horses in the woods near New Smyrna, we came across what looked to be an abandoned car, but when we drew nearer, we saw the car was rocking. My cousin had to explain to me later that there was a male and female having sex in the car. It hadn't dawned on me until now, why they were hiding in the woods to engage in this intimate activity. Shame! So, so many things are only taboo to talk about, yet they happen every single day. Some examples include child abuse and molestation, incest, rape, pedophilia, domestic violence, child marriages, genital mutilation, child sex trafficking, mental "illness", causes of poverty, genocide of the Native Americans, and the list could go on. Isn't it interesting that the dynamic is that the victim feels shame for what an offender did? Thinking back to my childhood, I remember coming home from church one Sunday and rather than go change out of my Sunday dress, I decided I would go play with some of the neighborhood kids, all of which happened to be little boys who were slightly older than me. On this particular Sunday, they had devised a new cruel prank to play on me. Two or three of them had decided to urinate in a cup and tell me it was Mountain Dew soda, in hopes I would drink it. I wasn't falling for it, but since I wouldn't drink it, they threw it on me. Rather than go tell a responsible adult, I did what any abused child would do. I immediately reacted with shame. I hid in the backyard and hosed myself off and sat waiting to dry in the sun, crying, feeling victimized, but rather than talk about what happened, I internalized the shame, which in turn protected the bully offenders. This dynamic is all too common. This is the dynamic that perpetuates the sick family secrets that destroy us, destroy our families, destroy our communities, which in turn collectively destroy nations and cause us to all lose touch with our humanity. How is that? How is *not* "airing dirty laundry" an act of benevolence? In our society we have replaced real kindness with "being nice." What's the difference? Being nice is sacrificing what needs to be said for acceptance, which does an injustice to all. When one is kind, things that need to be said are said, which keeps the sender of the message in integrity with their self-worth, while in turn holding the receiver accountable for their behavior. It has become painfully obvious that neither self-worth nor accountability are on the top of people's agendas, but there is hope. This can be changed on a grand scale, but first it must start with each individual.

There is yet another detrimental effect of not speaking the truth of what happens to us. When we internalize this shame, we start to blame ourselves. When we perpetually blame ourselves, we begin to hate ourselves. When we hate ourselves, we treat ourselves in an oppressive manner. When we oppress ourselves, we hate ourselves even more, but are not always conscious of why. Until we begin to become aware of and take responsibility for these cycles, we will continue to perpetuate them. And the painful truth is that these cycles do not end with us. These cycles are subconsciously passed onto our children and perpetuated amongst our peers, allowing these cycles to become even more fortified and more widely accepted as the norm. That's exactly how these conditions become the societal norm. If you can ask yourself, "am I ok with living in a society that encourages and embraces shame, blame, lack of accountability and lack of responsibility?" and your answer is "yes," then you need look no further. However, if you ask yourself this question and the answer is "no," then you need to look inside yourself to see how you are actively or inactively perpetuating these themes in yourself through your internal dialogue or perception. In what ways have you become indifferent to these qualities?

When there is a lack of healthy communication and the things that need to be said are suppressed, they will eventually come out, often in the most inconvenient and inappropriate ways. One such incident in my childhood is a clear demonstration of this fact. Talking about feelings and emotional needs was something that wasn't done in our family. We were kind of the "you want to cry? I'll give you something to cry about" type of family. My attempts to express hurt and disappointment were never welcomed. In fact, they were often met with blame and excuses. Generally, the blame was directed at me. When the time came that my Mother became so chronically ill that she could no longer work, she was left with no choice but to sell my horse. I was of course heartbroken. That was what I looked forward to every weekend. It was the one thing that I had that the other children in my school didn't have. It was the one thing in my life that made me feel truly alive and loved, loved by the horse and loved by my Mother. When she broke the news to me that she had to sell "Sarge," I was devastated. I probably said some really hurtful things to my Mother. After all, I was ten years old and lacked the emotional maturity that I now embrace. She was taking me over to my best friend Jessica's house for a sleepover. Whatever was said in the car was obviously not resolved and ended on a bad note. Hours after she had dropped me off, so late in the evening that Jessica's mother and younger sister were already asleep, there was a loud persistent knock at the door. Jessica and I were up in the family room watching a movie. Afraid to answer the door, we waited for her mother to get up to see who it was. Once her mother, Denise, opened the door, there stood my Mother, angry, tearful, possibly drunk. She slurred, "where's my daughter?" Denise stepped aside and my Mother stepped in the door. She began yelling at me stating what an awful, selfish daughter that I was, that if I thought she was so terrible, then maybe she should put me up for adoption. I don't remember the exact words or the order in which they were said, but I do remember that horrible feeling, the feeling of being completely unwanted and unloved, not to mention the shame that came with other people knowing that I was unwanted and unloved by my Mother. This has been a topic brought up in therapy again and again for years. Many Eye Movement Desensitization and Reprocessing (EMDR) sessions have focused on this memory alone. Denise, who by profession was a psychiatric nurse, did her best to deescalate the situation and send my Mother away. Not having a healthy flow of communication meant that that incident was never spoken of again between my Mother and me. When I returned home, it wasn't brought up; there were no apologies, no amends, no validation. At the time, I think I was too traumatized to react; I was frozen. Not having the ability to process such emotional trauma at that age, I suppressed it into the subconscious mind, the storehouse of all things that we can't or don't want to consciously face. Although memories like that are not consciously thought about, we continually react to them nonetheless. In fact, it may be the subconscious that unwittingly has the most influence over who we are and who we become.[1]

After years of working on myself, healing from the inside out, and many hours spent with EMDR therapists, I am finally able to look back on my childhood and see the positive, loving experiences rather than just the painful, traumatic ones. I am not disclosing these memories to identify blame or fault, as those two things are completely unproductive, and even more destructive. I am and will be simply pointing out these truths as a basis to build upon and identify solutions, solutions

---

1   "EMDR is an integrative psychotherapy approach that has been extensively researched and proven effective for the treatment of trauma."

to the social feature in our culture that are at the root of these problems of American families. I recognize that my family did the best they could with what their family provided them, as these are obviously themes that have run through my family for generations.

I further recognize that although any abuse is traumatic, as is poverty and all of the social nuances that are included in it, but the fact is even the poorest of the poor here in the United States in no way are comparable to the poorest populations in third-world countries. After all, there is still a considerable size of the world's population that goes without clean drinking water. Just imagine being faced with the choice of dying from dehydration or drinking water that is most likely diseased and may cause you to contract an illness that could cause you to die anyway. What a choice! If every human life is of value, no human should ever be faced with that decision.

So, the question that has come up again and again in my mind: what are the factors that attributed to my being "at risk" as a child? I believe that there are five main areas of child development: physical, emotional, intellectual, spiritual, and sexual. My physical needs were met. I was given more than adequate shelter, food, and water. My intellectual needs were met; in fact I was encouraged to excel in that area. I would say my spiritual needs were met, as my Mother and Grandmother greatly attributed to and encouraged my growth in that area. The areas that were greatly underdeveloped or had deep dysfunction were the emotional and sexual areas. How could those areas be fulfilled when my caregivers had never been healthy in those areas themselves? Every one of them had been victims, perpetrators, or both.

I believe that in order to resolve problems, one must approach the issues with a solution – focused mentality – but how can one find appropriate solutions without first clearly identifying the problem? The problem within my family dynamic was the type of secrecy that is the result of shame. I know that my family is not unique in this way either, that this is common in many families...so common that this may even be a societal epidemic.

3

The Formative Years

"It is a mother's influence during the crucial formative years that forms a child's basic character. A home is a place where a child learns faith, feels love, and thereby learns from a mother's loving example to choose righteousness."
- Ezra Taft Benson

MANY CULTURES HAVE a "coming of age" party, celebration, ritual, or ceremony to celebrate a female child who is leaving their girlhood and entering into the journey of womanhood. In Judaism there is the Bat Mitzvah. In highbrow Western culture there are Debutant parties. In the Mexican culture there is the Quinceañera, and the Lakota have the Ashnati and other Indigenous cultures all over the world have some way of honoring this rite of passage in a woman's life. Unfortunately, many women do not get to experience or be recognized for this honor. Some choose not to; others are never offered the chance. Even more unfortunate are the situations in which young women's innocence was stolen from them far before their minds and bodies were matured enough to receive such an action. Such was my case; my

"Coming of Age" collided with my Mother's social life and descent into drug addiction.

There are three responses of the parasympathetic nervous system: fight, flight, or freeze. When abuse begins at an early age for a child, it seems that the initial response and the one that becomes conditioned is the "freeze" response – at least that is what was true in my case. When I was being violated, I froze. As a child when I was being violated at night, I lay there and pretended that I was still sleeping. It felt safer that way, like if I pretended it wasn't happening, maybe it would all just go away. That reaction stuck until the age of twelve or so. The anger that I had internalized toward my Grandfather began manifesting outwardly. There was one such occasion when a friend from school was over at our house and my Grandfather said something especially cruel and hateful to me. I grabbed a butcher's knife from the kitchen and began to charge into the living room. My friend Chrissy stopped me and shook me out of my state of rage. That was my first experience of fight. There was so much anger inside, I could no longer contain it. Shortly after I was in the office with my Grandmother talking to her and I brought up that I felt like my Grandfather had done something awful to me, implying that he had been molesting me. My Grandmother became so upset with me telling me to never utter words like that again, essentially implying that I was lying. It was then that a huge void was created between myself and the person that I felt the closest to. In retrospect, this was a certain foreshadowing that the fighter inside *had* to awaken. The person that I trusted the most and expected to protect me had just shown me where her loyalty lay. I was left alone to fight my own battles.

By twelve years old, the abuse that I had internalized for years began to be expressed outwardly. My rebellion became very outwardly obvious, so much so that the other "troublemakers" that I associated with thought that I took things too far. On one such occasion I was going to a party in the seventh grade while I was still attending Catholic school. I knew that there were going to be freshmen from a local high school attending, so I wanted to make a "good" first impression. The party was also being thrown at a friend's family home. At that age, I thought they were rich – a home on the golf course, a Lexus in the driveway. In retrospect, I realized her parents were most likely divorcing as a result of money problems from the debt they were in as a result of their spending habits, but that is neither here nor there.

The point of the story was I wanted to make an impression, so I went to my Mother's drug dealer roommate, Dean, and his girlfriend, Lisa, and asked them for some pot and if they would go to the liquor store and buy me a bottle of liquor, saying that I needed enough to take to a party. How does a twelve-year-old have enough money to buy weed and a bottle of liquor? Probably from babysitting, or some other side job that a twelve-year-old would have. Maybe I had an allowance at that point; I'm not actually sure. Maybe Dean and Lisa were just giving these things to me, starting the "grooming process." All I know is I went to this party with a half gallon of vodka from ABC Liquors, cigarettes, and a cellophane with weed in it. Once I got to the party, I got the "cool kids" together, the ones that I wanted to impress the most, and we went out to one of the sand traps on a golf course in MetroWest. We all lit up our cigarettes, but when I broke out the other party favors everyone seemed shocked. I even recall my "friend's" older sister, one of the high school freshmen, touting, "That's not cool! I'm going to tell Mom."

Going back to the party, I was crushed. I thought surely, I would have gotten more acceptance from the self-identified "freaks," the Marilyn Manson, Nirvana, and Hole fans. After all, the majority of the alternative music scene was all about using, or at least that was my perception and experience. I think maybe one or two of the other teens may have stayed to take a sip or two of the vodka, but in the end, it was me by myself out in the sand pit, drinking alone, seeking to numb that pain of rejection. If I didn't already have enough signs that I was an alcoholic, even at that young age, this would have been another big indicator. I sat and drank until I was drunk. I stumbled back into my friend's home, headed straight for the bathroom adjacent to her bedroom, and vomited. I hid in her room for the rest of the time that I was there and waited for my Mother to come get me, when she could take a break from getting high.

It was at this time that the way in which I dressed dramatically changed as well. I went from just wearing the band t-shits that I liked, to imitating the musicians in the bands themselves – ripped jeans, fishnets, punk rock hairstyles, heavy makeup and hair dye. This was subsequently the same year that my Mother had admitted to me that she used drugs. Since my Mother was more like a friend to me than a Mother, it was very easy for me to rationalize in my juvenile mind, "well, if my Mom can get high, why can't I?" From that point on, it became obvious that my Mother's and my relationship was more of a competition than anything else.

When I was thirteen, the popular thing for kids in the subculture I so badly wanted to be a part of was to go hang out on "the square" in downtown Orlando, the legendary Wall Street Plaza. It was located directly off of Orange Avenue. Technically it still is, but it certainly isn't the same place that it used to be back in the 90s. Located in this in-famous spot for teen runaways, punk rockers, gutter punks, "ravers," and Goths was a club named the Kit Kat Club, Subway, the office of Morgan, Collin, and Gilbert, and my personal favorite, the coffee shop named the Yab Yum. This was the location where teens and young adults, sometimes even the wayward and lost older adults from all over Orlando and the surrounding areas, came by bus, bike, car, or foot – whatever means of transportation was available – to come to-gether namely with one goal in common: to escape whatever hellish reality was theirs on the home front. Yes, maybe a few of them were what we called "house punks," kids that just dressed the part of one of us street kids, who really seemed to have all of their needs met at home. So, it was safe to say that the majority of us came from broken, unstable, abusive homes. A typical Friday night included catching the bus down to the Yab Yum, pooling our money together and "spanging" (spare changing) the money that we didn't have to purchase a vehicle for further escape. Initially cigarettes were my gateway drug, then al-cohol, then marijuana, and it progressed from there.

I remember the first time that my friends and I ever used marijuana. We had planned it for what seemed like weeks. There was one person in the group that knew a middle school student who sold weed at Robinswood Middle School. We all handed our cash over to make the purchase. We wanted to use for the first time somewhere special, somewhere where we would be recognized by the older, cooler in-crowd for this rite of passage. The backyard simply wouldn't do. We had to use on Wall Street Plaza. The plan was to roll up a joint and smoke it on the wall in the back past the cul-de-sac. It was the end of the school week. We all rendezvoused at the bus stop or met each other on the 28 bus to downtown Orlando. We got there; we reviewed the plan: once we were high, we would parade down Wall Street to the Subway to make "suicide" sodas with the first goal of being seen and the next goal of quenching our cotton mouths. We got to the destination. We had the weed, but there was one crucial detail that we had left out: a method with which to smoke it. We all searched our backpacks for something that would work, but being new at this whole getting stoned thing, we found no solutions. Then it dawned on one of us; dollar bills are made of paper! So, we executed the plan, rolling the worst joint ever in the history of pot smoking, in a dollar bill. Of course, we were all hacking our lungs out. I recall saying something like, "it's not working. I don't feel any different!" until we started making our way over to the Subway. That's when it hit our systems like a ton of bricks. We were *high! Extremely* high!

Looking back, I think it may have been more than just the marijuana, I think it may have also been the combination of the pot mixed with smoking the toxic ink of the dollar bill, after all, according to CNN News 90% of money contains trace amounts of cocaine. But it was just like the movies depict it, nearly identical to the scene in "Half Baked" when Thoroughgood , Bryan, Kenny, and Scarface all meet behind the store to get high and wander into the establishment and everything turned larger than life...the pop tasted better than it ever had before, and the jokes were funnier than they ever had been. Everything was downright hilarious. Not to glorify the act of kids getting high, but this was when the behavior served its purpose. It magically gave us a method of escapism to relieve the silent, comfortable suffering we had become accustomed to in our everyday lives at home and in school.

Wall Street was the place I first experimented with nearly every drug. Shortly after first using marijuana, my friends and I sought out the legendary drug from the 60s, LSD. We had decided to dose the drug while we were downtown and made it safely back to my Grandparents" house. My Mother noticed that we were on something, as it was very apparent. This was when I first confessed to her that I, too, was using drugs. Rather than reprimanding me for putting myself at risk and lecturing me about the potential dangers using these types of drugs at such an early age while the brain is still developing, she scolded me for using these drugs in public, in "unsafe/unmonitored" settings. The message was clear: if I wanted to use, I needed to use substances at home with my Mother.

Of course, the changes in behavior that go along with drug use were becoming more and more obvious to certain faculty at the middle school I was attending. One such faculty member stood out and still has a place in my memory today, Ms. McPeak. She was the school guidance counselor. She was younger than all of the staff, fair skinned, with blonde hair, but the quality that made her stand out the most is that she actually seemed to care. She was the type of professional that put people before policy. One such example of this was one of the times that I had skipped school to go downtown with some of my friends. We were picked up for truancy and returned to the school. The school policy on truancy dictated that if a student currently had an extracurricular class on their schedule, they were to be withdrawn from that class and placed into another academic class. Since I was still able to maintain A's despite my erratic attendance, was enrolled in all of the advanced education classes, and my extracurricular class was assisting in the classroom for students with learning disabilities, Ms. McPeak decided to give me another extracurricular class instead. She assigned me to the Guidance Office to be her assistant. I never asked why. Maybe it was because she wanted to keep a closer eye on me. Maybe she saw my potential and hoped to influence me for the better. Or, maybe it was because she had no other choice and simply made that decision by default. I was assigned to doing some form of data entry-type work where I was given access to one of the computers in the office. Rather than just doing the work that I was assigned, I took it upon myself to figure out how to change the grades and attendance records for myself and some friends. Of course, I thought that was the "coolest" thing back then; however, now I recognize that I completely lacked the reciprocity and respect for an individual that went out of her way to help me. I don't think that I was ever caught, nor did I ever admit to this act of violating her trust in me. Even after that she recommended me for the new dual enrollment program that was just starting up in the county. I was eligible for a full scholarship for my college tuition, books, and transportation to the local community college. I was so excited at the thought of attending college at the same time that I was starting high school. The only catch was that I needed parental permission, and that required my Mother showing up for a face-to-face meeting with Ms. McPeak. My Mother never went, so that opportunity was lost. I was absolutely devastated. The belief system that I had adopted was only reconfirmed...why even try?

Looking back, I feel so much sympathy, empathy, and sorrow for the lost little girl that I was. I would now immediately recognize that a child acting out in the ways that I was, was simply a child starved of love and attention. It started with substance abuse, then truancy, then theft...the foundation on which more horrific events were soon to come. Being starved for love, it doesn't take Sigmund Freud to guess what deviant behavior was next on my agenda. I started "dating" in the eighth grade as well. This basically equated to hanging out, smoking cigarettes, eating fast food, and listening to punk rock and gothic music genres of the 70s and 80s. I was dating a rather strange character, who despite his awkward appearance intrigued many of us young girls due to his "legendary" status. He was infamous for the way in which he had landed himself in a local adolescent psych unit. Allegedly he had run over a cat with a lawn mower. For some reason we found this repulsive, while at the same time being fascinating. This boy had taken a liking to me, and being the love-starved girl that I was, I was immediately infatuated and so excited that someone wanted to give me affection. I had always been the "ugly duckling," so the experience of someone finding me attractive was enthralling. I would go over to his parents' apartment during the weekends while his parents weren't home. It was there in his bedroom surrounded by Misfit and KMFDM band posters that I was introduced to my first consenting experience of sexuality. I didn't technically loose my virginity, but I was introduced to what fellatio was. It was horrible. I was bad at it, and I felt dirty and used afterwards. To my recollection it never happened again with him and I refused to go any further. Shortly after came a very difficult lesson to learn at such a young age. If you don't satisfy someone's needs, they will find somebody who will. The only thing that we *needed* to be doing at that age was going to school and doing our homework! But again, I see now that we all were just looking for the love that was lacking in the broken homes that we came from. So this young man, not receiving the sexual gratification that he wanted from me, sought it out from one of my closest friends. I wouldn't give up my virginity to him, but she did.[2]

At the time, however, I was totally devastated. The rejection and betrayal hit so deeply on my young heart. Many depressing poems were written over it. But even more importantly I developed a very dysfunctional, yet widely and socially accepted view of sexuality: it's all about competition. I now believe sex to be a very sacred act, in fact I believe it to be the highest manifestation of spirituality, the sacred union of two souls, but my beliefs back then were completely contradictory to something spiritual. So, it was a competition, and the game was on!

I was introduced to a guy who attended the local high school. If I wasn't to be the first of my friends to lose my virginity, then I would be the first one to date an "older guy." His name was Lance and he was a

---

2   I will not disclose the identity of this friend, as she is still my friend, I love her dearly.

real jerk, but back then I thought he was the best thing. Knowing that at least one of my friends had already done the deed, I made it my goal to follow suit. One evening after school, Lance came over to my grandparents' house where I lived at the time. I spent a lot of time in my grandparents' bedroom, as this was the only other room aside from the living room that had a TV and a landline (this was of course way before every child had their own iPhone). Whenever I had company over, this is where we would spend a majority of our time unless we were out on walks smoking cigarettes or going to the McDonald's that was a few blocks away. The rule in the home (of which there were few) was that if there was a male friend there, the bedroom door had to stay open. Deprived of the essential attention and structure that children/adolescents require, I knew that this rule was easily manipulated. On this specific night, Lance and my friend Jessica from down the street were both over visiting. I probably told my Grandfather that I wanted to crank up the stereo so I was going to close the door, but since Jessica was there he thought he didn't have anything to worry about. This was all premeditated. I told Lance to bring a condom, told Jessica I needed her there as my "wing girl," and so it happened. Jessica hid in the closet and we did the deed. There was no intimacy, it wasn't special, there was certainly no love. It was just a mechanical act, purely motivated by my need to compete with my friends and have bragging rights. The next day, I distinctly remember going to school, meeting my group of girlfriends before the first bell rang and greeting them saying, "guess what I lost last night?" The reply that I got: "it's about time! We've all lost ours already." There was that same familiar sense of defeat. If life were a board game, which it is an actual board game, I lost again.

The summer after eighth grade was more of the same. More late nights in downtown Orlando, more experimenting with sex, drugs, and criminal behavior. My best friend "Chickee" and I had our first run-in with the law during our eighth-grade year. Aside from the truancy incident, at least the one where we were caught, we were caught shoplifting make-up from a local grocery store. We were caught by security, the police were called, and we were charged with trespassing. Our parents were called, and we were grounded. So, again, more of the same that summer. This was also when I discovered that my Mother was smoking crack cocaine. I had wondered why she had had such a dramatic change in her behavior. She stopped locking herself in her room and sleeping all day; she all of a sudden had "friends" and what seemed to be a social life. When I would inquire about what was new in her life, she always told me that it was the return of her old flame from her twenties, Rhett Baylor. She likened him to Rhett from *Gone with the Wind*. The only similarity that I saw was that they were both assholes. It turns out, however, that it wasn't just Rhett Baylor – it was Rhett Baylor and crack cocaine, and all the dysfunction that came with both.

I don't quite recall how I found out my Mother was smoking crack...it's highly unlikely that she was forthright about it. I am guessing I walked in on her or her friends smoking crack in our family's second home, which originally was my Great-Grandmother's house, then my Grandmother's art studio, then eventually one of the infamous crack houses of the neighborhood. My Mother, Susan, spent more and more time there, eventually moving up there, but just to give a little more background on that house, it had become a crack house long before my Mother moved in. My Uncle had lived there previously and had also been hooked on crack cocaine. As a child I wasn't fully aware of the behaviors and the details, but I was painfully aware of the results and the consequences. For instance, when my Uncle would run out of drugs and money he would come down to my Grandparents' house demanding more money, often resulting in a big yelling match between him and my Grandfather. Once when I was twelve, my new Gibson Epiphone Acoustic guitar went missing. No one seem to know where it was, but even at that young age I knew that it was the result of drug addiction. Years before that, my Uncle had gone to prison. At the time I didn't know why, but later I found out that it was a drug related charge. So yes, this house had a long haunting history.

If I am not mistaken, this was the summer of a significant loss in my life. My closest and dearest friend, even still to this day, was grounded for months and forbidden from ever seeing me again, so long as she lived under her mother's roof. My best friend, Jessica, who had been in my life since I was seven years old, was specifically told by her mother that she was not allowed to go downtown, due to all the mischief we got into down there throughout that summer. Of course, we developed a plan to get around that rule. She was to say that she was just spending the night at my Grandparents' house with me. We would catch the bus there and catch the last bus back around midnight and her mother would never know. However, her mother came by my house, most likely to check in on us and confirm that we were where we said we would be. And of course we weren't...that was the beginning of the end of our friendship. Hungry to fill that void of the person that I was closest to, I began searching for love in all the wrong places... again.

This is the part of my story that I experience so much fear of telling. It's my wall; my stopping point. As I mentioned in the beginning of the book, this is my third attempt of writing my story. I have never written this part. I have verbally disclosed bits and pieces to therapists and other trusted individuals in my life in recent years, but for the years before that, I pretended like parts of it didn't exist, in an attempt to pretend them away. Now that I have overcome the fear of facing these memories and allowing them to come forth from my subconscious. My only fear now is sharing them with you. Sharing this part of my life is my proverbial Brazen Bull.

The Brazen Bull was a torture device invented by a man name Perillos in ancient Greece. It was a life-sized brass bull crafted to look lifelike, even in sounds, movement, and the steam that would burst forth from its nostrils. The way in which this effect was obtained is quite horrific. The victim of the bull would be placed inside the hollow brass body, usually after having their tongue cut out. Fires were then built up around the body of the bull and as the victim would burn inside, the screaming and thrashing of the victim would cause the bull to appear alive. Once the critical temperature was reached resulting in the victim's body boiling, the steam would shoot through the bull's nostrils, further adding to the entertainment of the crowd. Ironically, the man who invented this device, who had expected to be greatly rewarded for his hard work and creativity that went into his invention, became the first victim of the device at the hands of the tyrannical ruler for whom he created it. In many ways, I feel that I have lived a good part of my life in the Brazen Bull, with my tongue cut out, unable to speak my truth, being burned by the fires of trial and tribulation, writhing in pain as my enemies look on in amusement.

But now is the time that I am making the decision to step out of that Brazen Bull, reclaim my voice and speak my truth before friend, foe, and stranger alike. Paradoxically I fear that by telling this part of my story I may be creating my own Brazen Bull, for which the courage and creativity it is taking to tell my story could possibly end in my demise, much as happened to Perillos. Either way I am making the decision to let my love of truth overcome my fear of death, so, I embark on my own perilous journey of unveiling the truth.

The beginning of the ninth-grade school year was a major turning point in my life. Nearly all of my friends had gone to other schools. Like the middle school that I had transferred to, I was in the ethnic minority. Not only was I in the minority, I was an outcast within the minority, and constantly the target of harassment and bullying. I could no longer focus on academics. I already knew the majority, if not all that they were teaching at that grade level, due to my love of learning and reading vast amounts of information at a young age, so I just didn't see attending high school as a priority. The last day I attended that high school, I went to school still under the influence of the LSD that I had taken the night before. The ugliness at the school that I had experienced through a sober perception became even more magnified. I was absolutely repulsed by the students, the faculty, the books, the entire education system. After that day I wanted nothing more to do with the public education system as I saw it as an indoctrination prison for the masses. I had found out about a Christian-based home school education system and urged my Grandparents to purchase it for me. My Mother went along with it, saying that she would administer the curriculum. I may have used the materials for the first month; however, my Mother was never really involved. She just didn't have the time with her "blooming social life." Later the materials and occasional tests just became a guise to avoid being considered truant.

Concurrently, the environment at my Mother's new "home" became much more relaxed in regard to using their drugs in front of me. In order to support her habit, my Mother allowed a drug dealer, Dean, and his girlfriend, Lisa, to move into the house. They paid their rent with the currency of crack cocaine. My Mother's boyfriend Rhett also lived there, and being the full fledged crack house that it had become, there were a slew of other characters, addicts and other drug dealers, that frequented the house. As my Mother distanced herself more and more from me, I found myself spending more and more time at the awful house with those nefarious characters. For years I beat myself up over that decision, as it seemed so stupid to expose myself to so much danger and devious individuals, but later in my life while studying the field of Applied Behavioral Analysis, I learned of a study conducted to observe the attachment behavior of baby ducklings that were exposed to negative consequences for seeking out the mother duck. Every time a duckling came within a certain proximity of the mother, they received an electric shock.[3] The hypothesis was that the behavior would be abated due to the negative consequences; however, the results of the study were quite paradoxical. The innate instinct of many mammals is to increase the behavior of seeking out love despite negative consequences. The less love we receive, the more we crave it, and our attempts to gain that love only increases. Of course, there are exceptions to this theory, but for me, it allowed a certain amount of compassion and forgiveness toward myself that I didn't have before.

The more time I spent around these people, the more I saw them using crack cocaine, the more curious I became about it. I would ask them what it felt like, why they liked it so much, why they always did

3   Modification of ducklings' filial behavior by aversive stimulation. Ratner, Alan M. Journal of Experimental Psychology: Animal Behavior Processes, Vol 2(3), Jul 1976, 266-284. http://dx.doi.org/10.1037/0097-7403.2.3.266

it. My Mother's new roommates seemed to have really taken a liking to me. They wanted to hang out. They liked a lot of the same music I liked. Lisa would share makeup tips with me and help me do my hair, something that I never really experienced with my Mother. I really enjoyed the nurturing and attention. What seemed like gifts of love, looking back I realized now were nothing more than a Trojan horse, something to gain my trust. This behavior is now referred to as grooming. One day at home, myself, Dean and Lisa, and my Mom's boyfriend Rhett were all sitting in the living room. They were smoking crack and I was watching. Out of nowhere, after Rhett had taken a hit, he grabbed my head and before I knew it had his mouth over mine, blowing smoke into me, something they called a "shot gun". I tried to pull away but he kept my face pressed to his. I was shocked, angry, disgusted, and felt violated, but within moments those feelings were completely wiped out by a sense of euphoria. Lisa gasped, "Rhett! Why did you do that?" to which he replied, "she wanted to know what it was like." Shortly after that, Lisa and Dean began offering me crack when they would get high. They became my best buddies. They were always willing to get party favors such as weed and alcohol for my friends and I and when my normal friends weren't around, they'd smoke dope with me. Initially my Mother didn't know. It was our little secret. Soon they started asking me to run "errands" with the men that they did business with. Initially I didn't want to, because I was scared and had a bad feeling, but I was quickly coerced into it. The first time I remember they wanted me to go get a fast food order with their dealer Sam, affectionately nicknamed "Candy Man." They reassured me that he had kids, he was a nice guy, and besides they *needed me* to go with him to get burgers from Krystal's up the street, because he always screwed up their order.

Hook ...line...sinker. I needed to be needed, I wanted to feel loved. In the short ride back from the fast food joint, "Candy Man" pulled out his penis and commanded me to "suck his dick". I turned my head the other way, scoffed and said "no," completely embarrassed by the situation. He grabbed me by the hair and forced my head down toward his genitals. Acting as though I may succumb to his command, I eased up on resisting. As soon as he let go of my hair and put his hand back on the wheel, I turned away quickly jumping out of the door of the moving van. Luckily we were in a residential neighborhood, so we were going slow enough that I was not injured. I ran as fast as I could to my friend's house. I never told her what happened because I was too ashamed, but later I did go back to my Mother's house and told Lisa, Dean, and my Mother. Lisa and Dean acted shocked. My Mother responded with denial.

Later, when I was walking through our neighborhood, Sam drove up in his other vehicle, possibly a Camaro, and he told me that if I didn't keep my mouth shut, he would kill me, to which I vehemently replied "fuck you, you piece of shit" after which he drove off. He continued to come to my Mother's house, and every time he would make some threatening remark, such as, "I'll catch you alone little girl," or some similar comment. Every time I would yell, "fuck you...." followed by whatever explicative I decided to call him that day. I was thirteen at the time. Several months later, while watching the local news, two of his sons, ages 10 and 13, had beaten and raped one of the female classmates in their neighborhood.

After this incident I never suspected Lisa and Dean being implicated in setting me up to be in that situation. I still trusted them and thought of them as friends. I basically looked up to them as role models, as I was lacking that influence in my life. They asked me to go on another errand with a man named Marty, whom they called "Daddy Starbucks." He was a business owner, and as far as I knew was not a dealer. I, of course, was more hesitant than the first time. Rather than just falling for the being "needed" trick, this time required being bribed. I was promised a bag of weed and $20 to go with him to the store with their "grocery" list and get what they needed. I was still hesitant and asked a bunch of questions, such as, "why can't you go? Why can't he just go alone?" for which they had sly answers to each. I allowed myself to be coerced and went with him. We went to the store and all seemed well. As we were leaving the store, he said he needed to stop by his house and grab something for Dean. He asked if I had ever been off-roading and I told him only on ATV's. On the way to his home, he cut off on a narrow road into the woods and drove recklessly in his SUV. Part of me was excited and part of me was scared. We got to his trailer and I said I would stay in the truck. He insisted that I come in, that he wouldn't be long and I could have something to drink inside while I waited. I was sitting in the kitchen of his singlewide trailer drinking a soda. He proceeded to ask me if I partied, to which I replied that I drank, smoked pot, and had tried LSD before. He asked me if I had ever smoked dope and I told him that I had a few times with Lisa and Dean. He proceeded to take out his crack pipe and a vile of crack cocaine and started to get high. I got high with him, but soon became uncomfortable and asked if he could take me home. He replied that we would leave soon as he started unbuttoning his pants and proceeded to rape me. For years when I recounted this story, I told people that he raped me by knife point, that he had cut me in the process as a result of my struggling and fighting so much. He did have a knife, but the fact is he never cut me and at some point I stopped fighting and froze in fear...he raped me until I bled. I went home in shock, bruised, sore, and bleeding. I went crying to my Mother and recounted to her what had happened and she responded the same way she always did...with denial. I was a liar and I was making the whole story up for attention.

In my underdeveloped, damaged mind, I came to the belief that it must have been my fault. Yes, I had made a series of completely irresponsible decisions that had gotten me into this situation, but in retrospect I was just like those poor little ducklings in that behavioral study. I wanted nothing more than love and acceptance and was willing to put myself in dangerous and self-destructive situations to fulfill that innate longing. But of course, I couldn't see that at the time. So I came to the conclusion that it was what I was wearing, which I still vividly remember. I had on a pair of cutoff jean shorts, a Nine Inch Nails t-shirt, and a pair of sneakers. It must have been the shorts. I carried that mentality with me for many years. Some of it was conscious, much of it unconscious, but for many years after that, I preferred to dress more masculine; baggy clothing, combat boots, military fatigues. I thought surely, I would be safe if I just altered the way I dressed. Of course, that false conception proved itself as just that. False.

It had become apparent that my Mother was completely consumed in the drug culture of crack cocaine. Her entire life revolved around it. The internal anger and pain that I felt was unbearable, so I sought out more and more relief. My escapism also included substances, just different ones than my Mother chose. By that point I hated crack and even more I hated crackheads. I hated being at my Grandparents' house due to all the childhood abuse and dysfunction that took place within those walls. My behavior became more and more erratic. I would stay out for days and weeks at a time living downtown, sleeping in parks, under bridges, and in abandoned buildings with other runaways and "throwaway youth." But even then, I didn't fit in. Having disclosed where I had come from, one of the other throwaways gave me the nickname "Crazy Crackhead Rachel."[4] I hated it, just as much as I hated the crackheads, including my Mother, who had abandoned, betrayed, and violated me. This only further added to my self-hatred.

Even among the other delinquent youth, I presented with an extreme case of anger, self- destruction and violence. I drank, I fought, and I did whatever drugs that we were collectively able to obtain. One specific night may demonstrate the level of hatred I had for myself. I was gathered under an interstate underpass with other delinquents, drinking whiskey and taking codeine tablets. When the other youth left, it was myself and a fellow in his early thirties nicknamed "Dogshit." It was common knowledge that Dogshit had AIDS and was a heroin addict. While under the bridge, as traffic zoomed above us, he took out his rig and stash of heroin. I begged him to rig me with his dirty needle; he would not. I begged him to have sex with me; he would not. Why would I want such horrible things for myself? I hated myself, I hated life. Part of me hoped that I would just die from a heroin overdose,

---

4   "Rachel" was the name I was given at birth. The origin is Biblical and Hebrew, meaning "ewe". I chose to change my name during my healing process to reflect the fact that I could make sacrifices but I no longer was a sacrifice.

the other part of me thought that if I contracted AIDS, then whoever raped me next would get what they had coming to them. My mind was broken, but even more so, my heart was broken. That night I would just have to be satisfied with the escape that came from the whiskey and the codeine. By this time, I was fourteen years old.

We both passed out under that bridge in a whiskey and opiate in-duced stupor. Shortly after, I was awakened by an unknown man who was sexually assaulting me. I attempted to wake up Dogshit because I knew he would protect me. In some dysfunctional way, he thought of me as his little street sister. However, he did not wake up. He was completely sedated by the effects of the whiskey and heroin. I realized that if I didn't do something, this unknown man would rape me, maybe even kill me. I began to feel around on the ground for something, any-thing that I could defend myself with. Finally, I found a decent sized rock and hit the man on the side of his head, hard enough to stun him. I scrambled out from under him and began kicking him as hard as I could. He rolled down the hill and took off.

The next day, I told Dogshit what had transpired the night before. He felt terrible that he was too incapacitated to protect me. We went and "spanged" (spare changed) enough money to go buy ourselves a couple of quarts of Old English 800 to drink off the effects of the sub-stances taken the night before. By the time we finished our beers we were hungry, so we decided to go to The Daily Bread, a local rescue mission, to get a meal. As we approached the mission, I saw him – the man who had assaulted me the night before. I immediately told Dogshit. He told me to go across the street and wait. From across the street I watched Dogshit give this man a good beat down, while yelling at him, screaming at him that he was a pedophile and he should keep his hands off young girls. As dysfunctional as this situation was, it was the first time I felt protected, defended, and loved.

I could go on and on about the various misadventures of my street life, but the highlight is that it gave me a sense of belonging and love that I had never experienced. We looked out for each other. We worked collectively to obtain food and substances to numb the pain that was a result of wherever we came from. Many if not all came from broken, abusive, dysfunctional homes. We were the lost children and the throwaways of society – the misfits, the rejects. We had lost our places in our homes and in our schools, but we created a home with each other. Granted, the home was only metaphorical; there were no walls and no roof, but we found a "home" with each other.

Among these throwaways, I met an eighteen-year-old, heavily tattooed guy named Cain. I was immediately drawn in by his extreme bad boy image. He was a military school reject. He had a skeleton hand tattoo over the top of his left hand and a dragon tattoo that he had just gotten that covered his entire head, among many other tattoos. I was immediately infatuated, most likely because on a subconscious level I knew he would provide me with the abuse that I believed myself worthy of. I unconsciously decided that I would do anything to win his love and acceptance. Believe it or not, I would be a victim of that very belief system, with that same individual on and off for fifteen years of my life.

We were sleeping in an abandoned building, downtown, like we did many nights. However, that morning was different. We were awakened early by a police raid on the building. Most of the delinquents escaped being apprehended by the police. I, on the other hand, did not. I was taken to the downtown police substation, charged with trespassing, and my Mother was called to come pick me up.

A couple of hours later my Mother arrived with her boyfriend Rhett to pick me up. She was very upset with me, not because I was endangering myself or that I had gotten in trouble, but more so that I had caused an inconvenience in her objective of getting and staying high. I was a buzzkill. She decided it was time to lay down the law and she was going to set rules and boundaries. By this time, I had no concept of rules, boundaries, discipline, or respect, and I certainly was not going to listen to anyone who completely lacked those things in her own life. Nevertheless, I was grounded, put on a civil house arrest. Her crack house became my civil prison. At times it was like a war zone. My Mother's mood was extremely labile. Often there was screaming and throwing objects. Commonly there would be little or no food in the house. I recall several occasions when I was either making a sandwich or pouring a bowl of cereal and my Mom would storm out of her room yelling at me for eating, that she had gotten that food for Rhett. Back then I just justified my Mother's behavior as her being a "stupid crack head," but now looking back, my heart aches. My heart aches for my Mother, that she allowed her fear of being in pain and alone to control her life to such an extent that she created what she feared most, while simultaneously hurting the people that loved her the most. And my heart breaks for the younger version of myself, the developing young woman that so dearly needed a Mom to talk about new life experiences and new emotions with, the young woman who received the message that she was not worthy of love, support, or protection.

I tried to maintain the best that I could in the insanity of that environment. There were drug deals being done literally around the clock, prostitution, firearms, and other countless examples of criminal activity. By this time, I had gotten my room back. I did my best to make it my "safe haven," which only meant that I had the music blaring and the door locked. Since I was obviously the most unsupervised of any of my teenage cohorts, all of my runaway, homeless, druggy friends knew where they could come and not be "harassed." At the time I considered this detail to be a fringe benefit of the whole situation. The reality of it was that we did have some epic parties and it was a much safer alternative to crash there than risk a trespassing charge from sleeping in an abandoned building.

One afternoon I had come home to the war zone to find Marty, the man who had raped me, in my room. Apparently, my Mother had allowed him to *clean my room*. When I walked into my room, he was sitting on the edge of my bed, reading my journal: my private thoughts, my sketches, my *poetry!* I was enraged. I snatched my journal from his hands. In response he made some comment about my writing, but I couldn't understand the words; hell, I could barely see him through the color red. As he got up to leave, he made the comment that I was a messy, messy girl, seemingly indicating my bedroom, but no doubt doubling as a perverse sexual innuendo. I screamed at him, pushing him out my bedroom door. I did what any other "normal" teenage girl would do; I slammed the door, blared the music, sobbed, and screamed loudly into my pillow. This couldn't be my life...I had to get out of there. I just couldn't take the insanity of that environment any longer.

Rhett had a close friend named Jimmy, a big, larger-than-life Native man. Jimmy had a family, a wife, and six daughters, five of which were still very young and lived at home. Jimmy and his wife Vicki ran a business together installing custom hardwood floors. I had overheard that they were looking for a babysitter for some evenings throughout the week. I looked at that as the perfect opportunity to get out of the house, earn money, and be in a more positive environment. It was great at first. I was spending the majority of my time there eventually and even started going to work to lay hardwood floors with them a couple of days out of the week. I was learning a lot of new skills, I was taking good care of their daughters, and I felt needed and loved. But eventually this place became unsafe as well. Jimmy was a crack addict and an alcoholic. He was a functioning one, but one, nonetheless. When Jimmy was high and drunk, he had the tendency to be a very angry man. On occasion he would come home and beat Vicki. One night I tried to intervene. As a result of his reaction I was afraid for my life, not because he threatened it, but because I did not recognize who he was in this state. He was volatile, impulsive, and violent. The girls knew from experience to stay in their rooms, but they surely heard everything that was going on, certainly for much longer than I had. I tried to ignore it, but was incapable of doing so. I had to leave, as the violence had just become too much ...so back to my Mother's house I went.

Shortly after moving back to my Mom's house, I was sitting in my bedroom with a couple of friends one night when I heard something at my window. When I pulled back the curtain, I found Rhett loitering in one of his drug-induced states of paranoia. I called for my Mom to come get her "stupid boyfriend." It turns out that this wasn't one of his normal states of paranoia. His friend Jimmy was outside...in the van...dead. He and Jimmy had allegedly went and scored some crack, heroin, and a prostitute; by that time I had learned that those were the typical party favors for this specific crowd that frequented the "Crime Hills" area. According to Rhett they all had gotten high and he and his lady friend assumed that Jimmy was simply passed out from the heroin. They did what any run good addict would do...picked his pockets and continued driving around getting high for hours. As soon as Rhett realized that Jimmy was dead, he drove to my Mother's house. I have no idea what they ended up doing. I assume they just dumped his body off at the hospital fearing any ties or police investigations. Any loyalty to friendship or family seemed to go out the window once addiction took control.

As I watched my Mother dive deeper and deeper into the lifestyle of crack cocaine and addiction, my heart sank with shame and despair. She had begun prostituting herself to some of the drug dealers that frequented the house and participating in other crimes with her drug-addicted associates. To cover up my pain and despair, my Mother became the punchline of jokes that I would share within my circle of friends, but then there were times that I could not hide the grief of a little girl who longed for her Mother. Those were the times that I would sit outside of her bedroom door and weep shamelessly, crying for my Mom. Often those cries were ignored, or even worse yet, met with annoyance and anger. Very seldom if ever did I get to see that caring, compassionate Mother that I once knew as a child. Crack cocaine had stolen her from me.

On one such occasion when I was outside of her bedroom door crying, I was approached by a man named John. By this time in my life I was very suspicious of the seemingly caring intentions of others, but John was different. John had been a family friend since he and my Uncle were children. My Grandmother had been their Cub Scout leader. He was a business owner and despite his addiction, still seemed to be a somewhat responsible, caring human being. He asked me what was wrong and listened. He took me out for some food, because as usual, there was none in the house. He didn't hurt me at that time; in fact, he gave me the care and affection that I craved. Whenever John would visit my Mom's house, I would spend time with him. He seemed to be the only person that "got me." Whatever I wanted he would supply, whether it was marijuana, alcohol, clothes, or food. He was there to support my needs. This process is now known as "grooming". Eventually, I started smoking crack cocaine with him. On one of these occasions he invited me to come to his house, and being that he had gained my complete trust, I obliged the invitation.

John lived in a very large home on Bear Lake in Apopka, Florida. He drove a new Ford Bronco XLT. He had a swimming pool with a beautiful tile mosaic of a mermaid on the bottom of it. He wanted for nothing. He was the most financially and materially sound person that I had ever known. His house felt comfortable and I longed to be surrounded by comfort. That afternoon we sat at his house and got high on crack, higher than I had ever been. I felt like I was going to lose my mind. I couldn't go back home in that state. I had to stay longer to come down. We sat in his living room and talked incessantly, as one does when high on stimulant drugs. I don't remember how the conversation started out, but I do remember the part of the conversation that changed my life forever. John stated to me that he was an undercover narcotics agent with the Drug Enforcement Administration (DEA). When he first said that I called bullshit, but then he produced a badge and what appeared to be a service pistol to prove it. He said that he had been busted years before and to get out of prison time, he cut a deal to work for them turning in other major players in the drug dealing industry. He told me that when my Uncle had gone to prison when I was younger, it was he that had set him up in a drug deal. He proceeded to tell me that I now worked for him and if I didn't do what he said that he would do the same to my Mother. At first, I retorted; I refused. His rebuttal was that being a whore was my birthright; that my Mother was a whore and even my Grandmother was a whore. I knew that he spoke the truth about my Mother, that she had been prostituting herself, but my Grandmother! "Fuck you!" I yelled, "You're a liar!" He continued to explain to me that because she sold out on her culture and committed her life to a white man that abused her and her children so that she would be financially supported, that qualified my Grandmother as being a whore. He said that she had once been a incredibly talented, independent, intelligent woman who sold her soul for material support. In my altered mind, his words started to make sense. I hung on his every word. I decided that he was right; I was no good. He had to be right; I didn't feel loved or cared for and that must have been the reason why.

From that night on, for the next year, I worked for him. He would come and pick me up from my Mother's house and keep me for days or a week at a time. He peddled my body to other addicts and dealers. I was shuffled around to crack houses and hotels around the Orlando area and put on display like a bovine at a judging show, just another party favor to be used for the night. I was dehumanized and humiliated by the way they talked about me and parts of my body, not to mention the sexual acts that I was forced to do. The chemical torture and restraint that he exposed me to allowed to become an expert at just checking out; completely disassociating. I would lay there conscious, but not home. I was completely numb...not just numb – dead. I was completely dead on the inside. There were other times that he didn't sell me, when he would just keep me in his home and torture me sexually, chemically, psychologically, and emotionally. I guess this was how he got his "kicks," as he could no longer achieve an erection due to his having diabetes. He would play some of the most sadistic games. Some of his favorites were, "Let's see if this will make your heart explode," wherein he would fill a socket that he had crafted into a crack pipe, fill it with copious amounts of crack cocaine, and then force me to smoke it. One may ask, "How did he force you to do drugs? Did he hold a gun to your head?" in a sarcastic manner. Yes, several times he did. He also liked to wait until I was near psychosis from the drugs and being kept up for days at a time, go to the breaker box, turn off the lights in the house, and as I was frozen in terror at the kitchen table, he would creep up behind me and place the barrel of his gun to my head, while telling me there was one bullet in the revolver, then pulling the trigger a few times. I never knew if there actually was, but it didn't matter. I cried hysterically each time, begging for my pathetic life, half expecting that the next time he pulled that trigger that my brains would be splattered on his kitchen wall. He had other ruthless games that he played, but they all had one thing in common: I never knew what reality was and what wasn't and I never knew if I was going to survive the game.

There were a few times that I thought that I was going to be rescued, that someone might help me. One of those times was when my Mother first came to his house and started banging on his door, screaming, "I know what you're doing to my daughter, John. I'm going to call the police if you don't give her to me right now!" The first time this happened, we were in his bedroom. He turned to me and said, "You think your Mother cares? She doesn't give a fuck about you. I'll prove it." He then got out some crack cocaine from one of his many hiding spots and greeted her at the door. I could overhear him saying, "Here, take this Susan. Now, shut the fuck up and go home." A small part of me held on to the hope that she would refuse it, that she would push her way past him, burst into his bedroom, grab me, and take me away, like a protective mother wolf, but that hope quickly died when I heard her close the car door, start the engine, and drive away. I was beyond devastated and beyond all hope. This was my lot, and my Mother agreed to it. There were several other occasions where the same scenario played out and on each occasion, he was able to buy my Mother's silence.

The other occasion when I thought that I was going to get help was the night he sent me out with a woman named Teresa to put me to work in front of the Parliament House. The Parliament House was an alternative lifestyle night club and hotel located on Orange Blossom Trail near downtown Orlando, an area that was popular for prostitution. Teresa was assigned to handle me that night. Because it was a gay and lesbian club, she wasn't having much luck finding men to solicit me to, and gay women were typically the minority there. Finally, she found two bisexual men who apparently had a fetish for young girls. She told me to stay outside while they went to the bar for drinks and to rent a hotel room. Once they were out of sight, I took the opportunity to run. I was running up a street called Paramore. This was one of the most crime- and drug-infested areas of Orlando. As I passed by the lowest of the low-income housing projects and apartments, I witnessed people smoking crack on stairwells and front porches. A child that couldn't have been older than 10 years old emerged from one of these projects, approached me and offered to sell me some rock. I kept going. I was determined to make it to the downtown area and find help, but from whom? I couldn't go to the police; they couldn't be trusted, not after what this alleged member of law enforcement had done to me. I finally got to Orange Avenue, the main street in downtown Orlando, where many of the bars and clubs are located. I started asking people for money for the bus or a cab. My intention was to get somewhere safe. Where? I didn't know, as I didn't have too many options at the time, and among the few friends that I had left, I didn't want them to see me in the condition I was in. How could I ever begin to explain what had been happening to me? As I was asking people passing by for money, a young man in a small group turned around and called me by name, obviously unsure if it was me. It took me a moment to realize who he was. It was Lance, the boyfriend that I had lost my virginity to only a year earlier, and now he barely recognized me due to how strung out I was. I approached him, telling him how happy I was to see him and that I really needed help. He quickly recoiled with a look of disgust, saying, "What happened to you? Get away from me, junkie!" Off he walked, laughing and joking with his friends, presumably about me. At this point I was so deadened that I could no longer feel the pain of any type of abuse or rejection. I half- heartedly kept asking people for money, but it was too late to get a bus and it seemed like I was never going to get enough money for a cab. Where was I going to go after all? So, I kept walking, to where I don't know. Eventually Teresa found me walking along Highway 50. I think that I had decided that my Grandparents' house was the best option. This was a place that I could come and go as I pleased and where no one cared enough to ask difficult questions that I didn't want to answer. They were used to me being gone for days at a time, but on this night, I didn't make it there. Teresa took me back to John.

At times John would take me home and drop me off at my Mother's house, where I would spend a few days or sometimes a week or two on reprieve, but whenever John would show back up I would beckon to his call, remembering and being often reminded of his initial promise to put my Mother in prison if I didn't. I don't know if I ever called his bluff or said, "Fuck it! Go ahead and set her up, send her to prison." After all, why did I desire to protect someone so much that didn't show care and concern for me? I know now that it is very common for children to protect their abusive parents. In my mind, if I had had any part in my Mother going to prison and she found out, she would hate me forever, and I would completely lose the possibility of her ever loving me again. On one such occasion, when I was allowed to go home, it was the month of April, specifically the day of my Grandparents' wedding anniversary. We had plans for the family to get together and go out to dinner like we did every year. This year ended up a little different. Prior to the dinner, I went up to my Mother's house to ensure that she was getting ready to go. Often, she would lose track of time and responsibility while she was getting high. I didn't want her to disappoint my Grandmother, so I took it upon myself to keep my Mom on track. I find it funny that even during the most traumatic time of my life, my internal "overly responsible adult" was still more responsible than my Mother. As I was sitting in her living room waiting for her to get ready, I was playing cards with one of her friends who had come over to get high. As I was looking out the window, I made a joke that I must be going crazy because I wasn't even high, but I swore that I saw a cop hiding behind a tree in the front yard. I was neither high nor crazy; there actually was a police officer behind the tree with a rifle. Moments later, the house was raided by the SWAT team. We were all ordered to come out of the house with our hands above our heads and then tear gas was shot into the house. Apparently, there had been an altercation across the street that involved a firearm and a witness reported that they had seen the suspect run into the house. It was a false report, and the only thing achieved by the raid was killing a litter of newborn kittens with the tear gas. Despite my efforts to ensure that my Grandparents' anniversary was a successful one, it was ruined. With experiences of defeat such as this one, being able to come home wasn't much of a reprieve after all. It seemed like there was no escaping the insanity around me. It was everywhere.

There were also times that John would leave me in his home alone. He did, after all, own a business, so he had to make an appearance there once in a while. When he would leave, I would fantasize about an escape. I would sit on the dock and imagine a different life. I attempted to take out the little rowboat, but it had a substantial leak, so my plan to get across the lake wouldn't work. And again, what would I do when I got there? Often, I would just wander around this affluent neighborhood hoping someone would ask me if I was okay or if I needed help. Sometimes I would get the courage to knock on people's doors, but I never got an answer. On one occasion I walked out to the main road and hitched a ride back to my Grandparents' house, but it was only a matter of days until John came back to pick me up. The whole situation just seemed hopeless, because it was.

Eventually the situation changed. A customer by the name of Neil decided that he was in love with me and wanted to keep me. I am unsure whether he bought me or stole me, but I do know his plan was to get money together to take me to Kentucky to marry me, as he said at the time it was legal to marry a fourteen-year-old in that state. But drug users aren't good at either saving money or bringing plans to fruition. He toted me around everywhere he went, kept me high, and used me as an accomplice for petty crimes like robbing soda machines and burglarizing model homes. At first, I was under the impression that I stayed with him by choice. I most likely could have been diagnosed with Stockholm syndrome. After all, he treated me better than anyone had ever treated me before; he gave me roses, fed me steak and champagne, and comparatively was far less abusive than my last keeper. During one of our cocaine-fueled fights, he told me to go home to my Mother if I thought I was better off there. So I did. As it turns out, my Mother was attracted to Neil and knew that that was where I had been. This gave her reason to hate me more than she already did, she didn't even attempt to hide her jealousy. The girl inside me died even more; a part of me still hoped she would feel concern for my well-being. Once I returned to her house, the explosive arguments began immediately. Amid a heated argument, she threw a Pyrex pie plate at my head. Luckily, I dodged it; it broke on the wall and shattered on the floor. I left the house immediately, going to a house a few blocks away to stay where I thought I could safely get some rest. I had become accustomed to taking a handful of Tylenol PM to sleep when I had been up for too long and needed to rest. I typically carried a bottle in my backpack but realized that I was nearly out. A man named Donnie that I had previously known from my Mother's circle of "friends" lived at said house and offered me a long white rectangular pill that he said would help me sleep very well. It turned out that it was a Xanax pill, something I had never used before and knock me out it did. When I came to, my pants and underwear were around my ankles, I was sore, and covered in bruises from my ankles to my buttocks. Several of these bruises resembled handprints from where I had been repositioned when I was passed out. It was immediately obvious to me that I had been raped. I ran back to my Mother's house and tried to tell her what had happened. I told her what Donnie had done to me. She wouldn't believe that he would do such a thing; after all, he was a friend of hers.

I did exactly what the medical experts say not to do after being raped. I took a long, long hot shower and attempted to scrub off the shame. It didn't work. I wanted to escape all the horrible feelings that I felt, feelings so horrible they were indescribable. I started drinking the beer in my Mother's refrigerator while I sat outside of her room sobbing while she got high. The pain inside would not go away, but I needed it to. I broke a beer bottle on the wall and started using the jagged edge of the bottle neck to carve into my arm. As I sat there cutting and crying, Neil came into the house, standing over me. He said, "I told you, you were better off with me," and he took me back.

By this time, he had found a place that I suppose could have been considered a more "permanent residence," in a house with an elderly man who was terminally ill and self- medicating with crack cocaine. This man's silence was also purchased through the power of this drug. The house was on a cul-de-sac in a neighborhood off Pine Hills Road. By this time the honeymoon phase of this part of my ordeal was over. Previously I had believed that I had a choice to be with this man, but now I was only a mere possession, kept under lock and key in this dungeon of a home with double-key bolted doors, bars on the windows, windows that had been secured shut with screws and nails. A couple of times I attempted to sneak a butter knife into the bedroom in which I was kept, hoping that I would be able to unfasten the bolted windows, but even if I had been able to undo the screws, I would still need to find a way to pry out the nails and get past the security bars. Yet again, my plan to escape the insanity I was imprisoned by seemed hopeless. I felt as though I was going to die in that smoke-permeated house that was inhabited by the empty shells of soulless creatures that had once been human beings.

While I was held there against my will, I was introduced to a syringe filled with cocaine. I would lay there lifelessly as men would inject me with dirty needles. The feeling was so euphoric I often imagined that this was what it must feel like to die and enter the pearly gates of Heaven, if there was such a place, freed from all pain and suffering. But the question was if I did die, would I *go* to Heaven after all I had done and all the things that had been done to me? As much as I hoped for it, I didn't die. The torture continued.

On one occasion, Neil had passed out after being up for days. I found his stash of cocaine and took it, hiding it on my person. The next day when he awoke, I convinced him that there was none left, that he had used it all the night before he passed out from sleep deprivation. My hope was that there was enough cocaine for one fatal shot, and if I got the opportunity, I would deliver that fatal shot to myself, if I could steal a rig and figure out how to shoot up myself. That night Neil had plans to transport me somewhere. He had obtained an SUV and had a couple of duffel bags packed. For all I know we could've been headed to Kentucky to be married (supposedly the law there at that time dictated that 14 was the legal age of marriage, at least according to Neil). There was something different about that day. Maybe it was the fact that I had just gotten a good rest, that I wasn't being chemically restrained with narcotics, or because I had some strength from eating some food. One thing I am sure of is that the situation involved Divine intervention.

As Neil was loading me up into the SUV, he made a comment I found especially offensive. I retorted to him in such a way that resulted in his pausing to slap me, causing me to fall to the ground. That was the moment it clicked. That switch inside me was turned back on and I was ready to fight for my life once again, an aspect of myself that I hadn't seen in far too long. Neil began apologizing as he always did after he became violent. I told him that I just needed a second, leading him to think that I was still stunned from the hit and fall. I took advantage of that moment that he let his guard down by kicking him in the groin as hard as I could. As he was doubled over in pain, I charged into him with my body weight, successfully knocking him over, and ran. I ran faster than I have ever run in my life. I listened for the sounds of traffic to guide me to Pine Hills Road so that I could get my bearings. Once I made it to the main road, I figured it was best to get out of sight, so I began cutting through backyards, jumping fences, running from dogs. I had no idea if he was following me or not, but I didn't want to take the chance to stop and find out. My heart was pounding so fast I thought that it was going to beat right out of my chest. I was running on pure adrenaline and instinct. The only safe place that I could think to go was a drug dealer's house, one of the only people that I could think of that was protective of me. So that's where I went.

I hid there for what seemed like at least a day or two. My concept of time at that time was still very illusory. My first time leaving his house, I went back to my Grandparents for a reprieve and so that they would know I was alive. I took the chance to clean up and change my clothes. I spent maybe a couple of days there, most likely sleeping for the most part, but eventually, the memories of what I had been through started to surface and haunt my psyche. I had to get high again to numb the pain. I'm not sure how I had connected with them, or even who "them" was; all I knew was that they were other addicts who had the same goal as I did, to get high, and most likely numb the pain of whatever they had gone through that made their lives so miserable. While we were driving around Orlando on this mission, we were stopped by the Orlando Police Department (OPD). Although I was at a point where I already had a very heightened suspicion of law enforcement officers, I thought that I could possibly trust a female officer to help me. As she was arresting me for possession, I had tried to explain to her about all of the rape, torture, and being held against my will. She said very little, but her cold, heartless gaze of suspicion said it all. After she had placed me in the back of the police cruiser, she came back once more with her police report and opened the door to ask me what my occupation was. Before I could answer, she answered her own apparently rhetorical question. "Oh! That's right. A crack whore," she stated condescendingly with that same cold, heartless glare of condemnation. For that reason, the name Officer Merk will forever be branded in my memory.

I was arrested, processed, seen in court, and placed on juvenile probation. I can't recall who picked me up or how I got home, but from that point on I decided that staying with my Grandparents was most likely the best decision, despite all the anger I experienced living there as a result of my early childhood experiences. I stayed off of the heavy drugs and spent most of my time taking care of my Grandmother, whose health was declining due to an ulcer on her leg that had become infected. I spent more of my time making meals for my Grandparents and taking care of her medical needs in between visits from the home health nurse. However, now without being heavily sedated with narcotics, I started having recurring nightmares and flashbacks. I asked my Mother to take me to the liquor store. When she came back out from the store and got into the car with the alcohol that I had asked for, I blurted out, "I think that Granddad used to do bad things to me while I was sleeping when I was younger. I keep having these nightmares and I feel like I am going crazy." My Mother looked at me in shock. At first, I thought that she was going to tell me I was lying, just like the other times, but this time was different. Her eyes welled up with tears and she said, "That bastard did that to you *too?*" Part of me was enraged at the fact that she had left me alone with this sick man. The other part of me was relieved that she believed me and identified with me. We went and got drunk to numb the pain together, which sadly enough was probably the most bonding that we had done in years.

This drinking episode turned into one of my benders, where I just was not able to get enough of whatever substance to numb the pain, the fear, or the paranoia that one of the many men who had abused me would come back for me. I made it back to my Grandparents' house safely and returned to my bedroom. That's when it dawned on me that I still had that stash of cocaine hidden somewhere. I eventually found it. I thought about just snorting it, but that surely wouldn't deliver the lethal experience that I was hoping for. Then I remembered I had seen a vintage glass syringe at some point in my Grandmother's medical supplies, a piece of memorabilia that she had saved from WWII. I went to the kitchen and took down the box of medical supplies from the top shelf. The gauge of the needle was very large and unlike the hypodermic needles I had seen when I had been injected with IV drugs before, and it was as dull as a throwing dart in a bar billiard room, but I was desperate, so it would have to do. I did my best to reenact the ritual that I had seen done so many times. Over and over I missed the vein and ended up with huge bubbles at the injection sites where I had missed the veins in my arms. I finally made my way down to my feet and hit a vein. I went and laid on the couch in the living room, thinking that this may be the last waking memory I would ever have of my miserable life. The following day I awoke to a short, young Hispanic woman standing over me. She introduced herself as Julie Perez, my Juvenile Probation Officer. I had apparently missed my appointment to check in for probation. She was there to inform me that I was going to detox and if I didn't go with her willingly, that she would call the sheriff's office and have me picked up for violating my probation. As intoxicated as I still was, I knew that I had no room to argue; I could barely put words together to form a sentence. I knew I had to go.

The whole thing was a blur. I was accepted into the adolescent Addiction Receiving Facility, affectionately known by the youth as ARF. I was fifteen years old at the time. During my intake I did my best to recount what I had experienced over the last two years as well as the details of my childhood. I was barely coherent. Now, looking back through the lens of my experience as a professional in the behavioral health field who has done countless psychosocial intakes, I empathize with the person who had been assigned to do my intake, as it must have been extremely difficult to hear and even more difficult to follow. I do remember the distinct feeling of struggling to maintain consciousness during waking hours. I would fall asleep while sitting up in class, groups, free time, and counseling sessions. I recall thinking to myself, this must be what it feels like to have narcolepsy. My time there was like one long, surreal dream.

I was eventually accepted into a residential treatment program called Clarcona Pointe, an adolescent substance abuse program run by The Center for Drug Free Living. By that time I knew my diagnosis by heart. I was a poly-substance dependent, meaning that it didn't matter what the substance was and I was dependent on being high. What I didn't understand at the time was that I was self-medicating in an attempt to numb the pain from the trauma I had endured. I didn't know it, nor did the professionals who were experts in the field, as this discovery has been one that has only really surfaced in the last decade or so by doctors and researchers such as Dr. Amen, Dr. Knuckles, and Dr. Maté

I will never forget my first session with my counselor, a youngish white woman named, Diane. After getting situated in her office and getting a thorough explanation of what the expectations of the program were, she said something to the effect of, you don't have to hide behind that smile anymore, we know about everything, even the *prostitution.* I sunk within myself; I wanted to disappear. There was that dirty, awful word again and I felt just as dirty and awful as the word, even more so. It made me hate myself even more. I went into detail about the things that had been done to me about the various times that I was raped, the way that I had been tortured, the ways that I had been sold like a piece of meat, how I was held in a house against my will...all of it. The Orange County Sheriff's Office was contacted, and a detective was dispatched. The detective came out and took a report. I gave names and locations, to the best of my ability. The distinct memory I have from that is the glaring suspicion in that man's eyes and how he kept going back to how I had been using drugs while all of this was happening, as if I gave permission for all of these things to be done to me, as if I deserved it *because* I was a drug addict. That was the last time I ever saw that detective. There was no follow-up, no investigation, no justice. My words were not heard and what had been done to me didn't matter. I didn't matter.

It didn't take long for me to realize that all of the other clients in this residential program were admitted for reasons such as getting caught smoking pot at school, drinking and driving, or similar offenses. They all lived at home and had decent parents and were still in school. I was the only crack-addicted *prostitute* and I had to hide that part of my story at all costs. After that police report was taken, I never spoke of it again. After all, it was obviously my fault. So I hid that part of myself away, buried in shame, disgrace and self-hatred.

Not long after I had been admitted to the inpatient program, I received word from my Grandparents that my Mother had been arrested. At first, I thought it was because I told somebody what had happened and John fulfilled his promise to set my Mother up in a drug bust, but really, my Mom had been arrested as an accomplice in a robbery with some of her using friends. I hated myself and hated her more than ever. The things that I allowed to happen to me in the name of protecting her were all in vain. In retrospect, I think her being arrested and sentenced to two years protected me from the disappointment of her not coming to visit me or bring me clothes or other creature comforts from home like the other parents did for their children. At least there was a valid reason now aside from her not giving a damn.

The time came when we all had to do HIV education and testing. I met with the counselor and took the questionnaire that was given before testing. According to the questionnaire I was at an extremely high risk for having HIV because of all of the risk factors that I had been exposed to such as dirty needles, having been raped, etc. Unlike today's rapid testing, it took two or more weeks to get the results back. I spent that entire time fearing that I was HIV positive. For the first time in a long time, there was a part of me that wanted to live, but I feared that the results were going to bear news that I did not want to hear. I spent those weeks bargaining with Creator, which was probably also the first time I had prayed in years. Several weeks later the miracle came. I was negative for HIV.

Going to this treatment center was probably the best thing that had ever happened to me. When one is surrounded by dysfunction for so long, it becomes the norm. You tend to lose awareness that anything outside of that dysfunction actually exists. My experience in this program taught me that there was another choice. I learned about Twelve Step Recovery, teamwork and communication through ropes courses, and survival camping on hiking and canoeing trips. During the four almost five months that I stayed in the facility I was given chores, responsibilities, and leadership roles, I earned my GED and enrolled in college courses by the time I left at sixteen years old. I had grown a lot, but when I graduated from the program I was returned to the same environment. My Mother was still incarcerated, so I was released to the care of my Grandparents.

My Grandparents' health was declining rapidly. My Grandmother had lost her mobility after having her leg amputated. Along with her mobility she lost her desire to live. She was more depressed than I had ever seen her. She suffered in a constant state of despondence. My Grandfather's health was beginning to decline as well. This is about the time that he began showing the initial signs of Alzheimer's disease. I did my best to care for them, to apply the new skills I had learned, but I discovered at my young age that it is difficult to maintain personal changes when you surround yourself with more of the same. There were frequent arguments and eruptions of anger between my Grandfather and me. Despite attending the local community college, working a part-time job, going to AA meetings, and participating in outpatient treatment, I was using in no time. I couldn't escape physically, so I rationalized escaping through altering my consciousness. My broken mind and spirit had concluded that it had been crack cocaine that had been the problem and as long as I stayed away from that specific drug, everything would be okay.

I went through several different addictions in the following year: huffing glue, snorting and injecting heroin and cocaine, and eventually the drug ecstasy. The downward spiral was faster than I could imagine. I failed out of school, lost multiple jobs, and had my first car impounded within a week of owning it. There was a black hole where my Soul had once resided, a God-sized hole that nothing could fill. In very little time my need to be high could no longer be supported by the little bit of money I made working in restaurants, so I turned to crime. I had learned a lot by observing my Mom and her friends, all their hustles and schemes to keep themselves high, so I started to apply that knowledge myself. The easiest crime seemed to be identity theft and check fraud, so I decided to let my drug-using friends in on the knowledge. Between check fraud and hustling drugs, we maintained our need to be constantly high and keep ourselves sheltered in cheap hotels and trailer parks, adorning ourselves with new tattoos and piercings.

I was completely out of control by this point. Even my drug-addicted friends were warning me that I was completely out of control, that I was using too much. There had been times that I was so gone on drugs that they would dump me in front of my Grandparents' house because they didn't want to deal with an overdose. Once, I had consumed a lethal amount of a poisonous flower known for its hallucinogenic effects. It was all over the news that teenagers around the country were overdosing and dying from consuming as little as one petal of the flower. Fully knowing this, I picked every flower off of the plant and made a pitcher of tea which I drank the majority of. Once I began to experience the effects of my brain being poisoned, I blacked out and spent the next few days fading in and out of consciousness. I vaguely remember being dropped off on my Grandparents' lawn. My Grandmother informed me days later that I had been exhibiting extremely peculiar behavior such as when they found me naked in the kitchen eating donuts and talking into a banana as if it were a phone. Although the effects were darkly comical, the incident illustrated two very important facts: how little I valued my own life and the level of cognitive dissonance in my family. Despite my "peculiar behavior" and the obvious fact that there was something very wrong with me, my Grandparents rationalized my behavior with the theory that I must've just had a high fever. That's how we dealt with things in my family.

A blessing in disguise came on the day that I let my greed outweigh my criminal logic. I insisted on hitting one more bank; I wanted to break the record of how much we made out with in one day. My friend and I were caught in the act committing check fraud. I say that this was a blessing in disguise because the way I was using, I wasn't going to last much longer. The judge had grown so tired of seeing me in and out of his courtroom he was now ready to try me as an adult. I was facing five years in prison for the felony charges that I had against me. The day of my arraignment, I experienced another case of Divine intervention. The social worker who was the assistant director of the treatment program that I had completed was contacted – by whom I don't know – but she showed up that day in court and advocated for me. I will never forget her name or how I felt that day – Valerie Gaye, the woman who believed in me enough to fight for me, to fight for my future. She explained to the judge that I had been consistently failed by the system throughout my life, how I had fallen through the cracks, and how I had been set up to fail by simply being returned to the same dysfunctional environment that I came from. She proposed that the judge withhold adjudication on the condition that I complete the same treatment program again and find a different place to go upon my successful discharge. The judge hesitantly agreed to her plea. It was that day that I affirmed I wanted to be just like her. I wanted to see the potential in people and make a difference in their lives. I found myself back at Clarcona Pointe, my home away from home. It was the closest thing I knew to a family reunion. I knew and loved all of the staff there. I couldn't get enough of the home-cooked comfort food. I was like a sponge when it came to learning about recovery. I really wanted it this time. Since I already had my GED, I helped the teachers with tutoring the other clients. Since I was a veteran of the program, I showed all the new kids the ropes. I finally had some sense of self-worth and purpose. Four months later, I was graduating from the program again, but I didn't want to go. I think the only way they were able to convince to leave was by agreeing that I could come back and visit whenever I wanted to and that I could come a do a peer-run group once a week. My counselor had found placement for me in a program funded through the county called the Independent Living Program. I appeared in front of the judge again to provide evidence that I had successfully completed the terms appointed by the courts. The only problem was that I still was not eighteen, so I became a ward of the court and was sent to live at a women's homeless shelter until I was old enough to sign my own lease.

It was probably the best scenario that I could have been placed in; however, knowing what I know now about the nature of trauma and trauma recovery, it was detrimental to my personal path of healing. I was determined to turn my life around, though, so I made the best of it. The Women's Residential Counseling Center, the program where I was placed, was located only a few blocks away from the location of the first-ever AA meeting in Orlando. I took full advantage of that. My first ninety days, I attended three meetings a day. I had a sponsor and worked the steps, attended counseling and group therapy, attended my life skills groups and spent whatever free time I had reading self-help books and trying to learn how to meditate. I focused all of my energy on my recovery for the first three months. After the first three months of my stay at the women's center, I decided that I should enroll into school again, so I started attending the nursing program at the local vo-tech. That went extremely well until we started the section on phlebotomy, due to the use of syringes to draw blood. I quickly discovered what a trigger was when it came to drug cravings. I utilized that as an opportunity to learn symptom management around my cravings and pushed through that part of the curriculum. As I neared the end of the LPN program, I started my clinicals at a hospital where I had previously volunteered years before. I was shocked by the lack of compassion, the way patients were treated disgusted me. After being reprimanded several times for advocating for patients and observing the ways that nurses were treated by doctors, I decided that the medical field just wasn't where I belonged, so I never did finish nursing school. I decided to resume taking classes at the community college and pursue a degree in psychology.

Meanwhile, for work I decided to pursue employment at a tattoo shop located across the street from where I lived. I had always wanted to work at that place; after all, it was where I had gotten my second tattoo. After several weeks of following up on my application, I was finally called in for an interview. Ironically, in the interview, the manager disclosed to me that I wasn't his first choice; in fact, I wasn't his second or third choice. However, I was the only applicant that was persistent about following up and because I lived right across the street, he decided to take a chance on me. Apparently, persistence was one of my strong points, probably a quality that kept me alive despite all I had been through.

When I turned eighteen, I moved out to an apartment of my own, and successfully completed the Independent Living Program. I learned a lot via that program. I learned how to run a household, budget, balance my checking account, save money, pay bills, draft a resume, and perform wonderfully in job interviews. Basically, I learned all the skills one needs to be a functional member of society. However, there was one crucial thing that I was never taught...how to love myself.

I was able to maintain my sobriety for a while longer. I made it to just over a year. But eventually I became tired of declining offers to hang out with my co-workers. For once in my life I wanted to have a normal social life and be accepted, so I started to hang out with the other employees at the tattoo shop. I did well for a while, abstaining from alcohol when I would hang around with them, but eventually my mind rationalized the fact that I was eighteen, that I was responsible enough to manage my life, and therefore I was old enough to drink responsibly. That thought couldn't have been further from the truth.

4

A Pretty Vacant

*"You must give everything to make your life as beautiful
as the dreams that dance in your imagination."*
- Roman Payne

THE FIRST NIGHT I decided to drink again was a complete and utter catastrophe. The night started out great. The entire staff, including the owner of the shop, agreed to meet at Roxy's Nightclub. This was a swanky club that pro-athletes and members of boy bands frequented. One of the tattoo artists knew a bartender that worked there who would serve us top-shelf drinks all night if we each threw in twenty dollars. Top-shelf drinks? A swanky night club with VIP status? It sounded like a classy night to me. But if you are an alcoholic who is a binge drinker, have ever been one, or know one, then you know that "classy" is a status only reserved for the first hour, two hours tops. My behavior that night nearly resulted in my being fired...from a tattoo shop...while I was off the clock. That should give you some idea of how far from "classy" I got.

This incident was certainly a foreshadowing of how successful I was going to be with drinking, but my pride kept me from going back to the rooms of AA and admitting I was wrong.

I was determined to find a way to use substances like a "normal person". After all, I wanted to keep my past buried. I didn't want look at my pain. I had gotten the message loud and clear from society that what had happened to me was my fault and I already hated myself enough, so it was not possible to look at my past.

For a while my life spiraled out of control, but somehow, I managed to stay out of jail and stay alive. My townhouse was a party house, just like my Mother's crack house, but I had myself convinced that somehow, I ranked higher than that lifestyle because there was no crack cocaine involved. Insanity ensued, nonetheless. I rented out rooms in my apartment to drug dealers. Even though I worked legitimate jobs, I was still attracted to a life of crime. I had been given a desktop, printer, and scanner from my Grandfather as a Christmas gift to assist me in the pursuit of my college degree. I figured out how to use it to counterfeit money, small bills, because those went unchecked. To be honest, I got a lot of kicks out of it. I would catch stories on the news about how small counterfeit bills were being passed off all over Orange County, and I was the one responsible for it, which somehow gave me a strange sense of accomplishment.

Eventually, this lifestyle caught up with me. One day as I was walking to my apartment from work, four men in business attire walked up to my door presenting badges, stating they were detectives with the Orange County Sheriff's Office, and bullied their way into my apartment. They said that they were there to investigate my roommate, who was allegedly was selling heroin. I honestly didn't have any knowledge of it, nor did I know how to exercise my rights, so I stood idly by as the four men proceeded to search my apartment, without a search warrant. I told them that they would find my pot and bongs, which they reassured me was not what they were there for, and they kept their word on that note. One of the detectives sat down at my desktop and started poking around on my computer, the one on which I had been counterfeiting on. I felt my heart jump up into my throat and my stomach sink. I knew that if he found what was on that computer,

I would be spending time in federal prison. I attribute this incident as another example of Divine intervention. He either didn't see the minimized window that had the evidence of ten dollar bills that had been scanned, or he chose to ignore it. I highly doubt that it was the latter. They ended up leaving, having not found what they were looking for, and thanking me for my time and cooperation. After they left, I went over to the desktop and sure enough, there was the scanned currency in a minimized window at the bottom of the screen. Something told me that that was Creator screaming at me to get my act together, so I did. I kicked out the drug dealers, ceased my own criminal activity, and made the commitment to make an honest living.

I went on thinking for years that as long as I made a living, had a nice car with a standard car payment, had a reputable job, a townhouse on a lake, and pretty things, that I was okay. As long as I looked good to the rest of the world, it didn't matter what I felt like inside. The truth was I was dying on the inside. During the day I medicated myself with doctor-prescribed benzodiazepines and painkillers and at night I drowned the ghosts of my past in alcohol and occasionally the recreational use of cocaine. I justified my using by the fact that I had become a responsible, tax-paying citizen and since I was using substances "like a Republican" [Using drugs that are considered acceptable in upper echelon Caucasian social circles (alcohol, prescriptions drugs, and cocaine)], it was okay. After all, Rush Limbaugh was my idol at the time. I deeply identified with his hardened, calloused, cynical views and was probably just as judgmental and nasty as he was. My worldview was that if I could pull my act together, then anyone could, that people just needed to stop whining and pull themselves up by their bootstraps. Did I mention how miserable I was and how I was dying inside? One thing that I hold to be true now is that the content and quality of our relationships with others is an insightful mirror of what is going on within ourselves, including the beliefs that we hold about ourselves and the world in general. I have had two long-term intimate relationships with two men in my life, each lasting roughly around four years, each teaching me a great deal about myself and the way that I approached life.

Landon was my first love. The first time I saw him, something in me knew that I would love him. I was seventeen. It was my Grandparents' wedding anniversary and I believe that it was the last time my whole family would ever share a meal together again. My Mom had recently been released from being incarcerated. Both my uncles were there, my aunt, my cousin, my Grandparents, and myself. I had taken on the responsibility for booking the reservations at the restaurant; however, when we arrived at the steakhouse on our side of town, we discovered that I had booked the reservations at the other steakhouse across town and there were no available tables at the location where we were. Everyone in my family was frustrated with my mistake and thought the dinner plans had been ruined. At that time there was still a part of me that was an optimist. I encouraged everyone that we could make it if we hurried. We had the hostess call ahead and inform them that we were on our way and to hold our table. Knowing what I know now, there are no coincidences. Everything happens for a purpose, and coincidences are simply Creator's way of remaining anonymous.

While we were having dinner, a busboy came into the section of the restaurant where we were seated. He had bleach blonde hair pulled back in a ponytail and the physique of a high school athlete. I immediately felt my face turn red and began smiling uncontrollably. My aunt and my Mother took notice of my reaction, so my aunt, being the jokester that she is, went and found him in the restaurant and informed him of my taking notice of him. As we were leaving, he came back into that section of the restaurant flashing a sheepish smile and waving goodbye. At that time in my life I wasn't very adept at identifying emotions, but I knew that I felt more positive, maybe even happier, than I had felt in a long time. A year or so later a mutual friend introduced me to him.

He had immediately shown interest in me, but I wanted to observe him and take notes for a while, so I kept him in the "friend zone" for a few months. I don't think he had any clue that we had met previously, but eventually I asked him if he had once worked at that steakhouse, which of course he had. Eventually, at a New Year's Eve party, I let on to the fact that I liked him by kissing him at midnight. That was the beginning of our relationship. He eventually moved in with me and for the most part we had a good relationship, except for the fact that I still had this deeply dysfunctional part within myself that I yet had to reckon with. I was unable to really love him, because I still hated myself. I found myself repeating what I had learned from my Grandfather; to show love by providing and giving material items. Basically, I wasn't able to let him into my heart, because I still had not yet learned to access my own.

I believe that my inability to give genuine intimacy and love resulted in his being unfaithful. I felt like because of my commitment to him and how hard I worked to give him things that he owed me something. Rather than leave the relationship like a person with a healthy sense of self-worth would do, I tried to control him, to make him love me. This only pushed him further away, which only contributed to my own self-hatred. The more pain I felt, the more I attempted to drink the pain away. The more I drank, the more emotionally abusive I became. I did not recognize it at the time, but I was engaging in some of the exact same oppressive tactics that my abusers had used on me. I sought to lessen his personhood, to devalue him to the point that he would give me what I wanted — to be loved. It took years of introspection to accept this painful truth — that I had in fact become what I despised. The truth is, we all have aspects of ourselves that we would prefer not to own, that are excruciatingly painful to examine. This truth came to a boiling point in our relationship, at the point where he could no longer bear being subjected to my abuse, hostility, and insanity. He moved out and we started to see other people. I became obsessed with this rejection; however, at the time I was still unable to accept responsibility for my part in what caused our relationship to go bad. All I knew at the time was he was the sole human being that had shown me the most love and affection to date, and I felt like I was going to die if I didn't get that back.

One night we had tentative plans to meet. I sat with my room-mate playing Texas Hold'em and drinking pinot grigio waiting for his phone call. As it began getting later and later, my mind obsessed more and more over the fact that I was being rejected; that love was being withheld from me. I called his cell phone several times but got no response. My anger continued to build and as it did, I lost sight of any logic I possessed at the time. The best idea that I could come up with was to drive over to his place and find out why he never called me. I discovered what I didn't want to know – he was in bed with another woman. I became blind with rage, threw a cinder block through a sliding glass door and entered his home. When I saw that he was with a heavy-set woman, I became even more enraged as I had struggled throughout our relationship with my own weight and he had made it obvious to me that he preferred an athletic body type. I was aghast by this betrayal, without realizing that I was the one who was betraying myself. I was so full of rage; I have no clue what I said or if it even made sense. I proceeded to rampage through his house like an angry bull, breaking everything that I had ever bought him. In response to this, he attempted to restrain me, to which I responded with a physical attack. He escalated his efforts and had me pinned to the wall by my neck, my hands fumbling behind me searching for something substantial enough to pummel him with. As my panic began to rise from the sheer lack of oxygen from being choked, I finally felt a vase on the shelf behind me, a vase that he kept filled with coins. I grabbed it and struck him on the head, breaking the vase, coins flying everywhere. Stunned, he grabbed his forehead to stop the bleeding and said something like, "you crazy bitch, I'm calling the police." Completely in shock, I stumbled out to my car and just sat and waited for them to come.

I found myself in front of a judge again, this time as an adult, facing five years again for home invasion with an explosive weapon and aggravated assault and battery. I was released on bond. I distinctly remember the day I was released was a few days after Hurricane Katrina hit New Orleans. I was watching the event play out on my TV screen, thinking that this was the end. Seeing the suffering and desperation unfold both in my personal life and there in the Big Easy, I was convinced it was Armageddon. I dropped to my knees there in my living room and began to pray, bartering with Creator that if She just got me out of this situation and would spare humanity, I would do my part to make the world a better place however I could. Landon decided to not press charges and the state agreed not to prosecute me since the victim was unwilling to participate in the prosecution, so long as I left him alone. So, I did, and Creator had given me yet another chance to do right in my life. By this time, I had lost count of how many chances that She had given me. No matter how good my intentions were, I just didn't know how *not* to be destructive. I was simply a pretty vacant, a beautiful disaster, filled with pain and anger that I still had no idea how to heal.

A few months later, while driving home from work, I was hit by a drunk driver. There were a couple of things that were miraculous about this night. The first that I was *not* the drunk driver; the second was that if the impact of the accident had been a few inches closer to my driver's side door, I would have been crushed. The accident put me out of work for several months on short-term disability. I was in chronic pain. My pain management doctor had me on so many medications that I no longer needed to abuse my prescriptions to get high. The doses and varieties he had prescribed worked quite well to get the job done. No longer having an eight- hour work day meant that the only reprieve from my drinking came when I finally passed out drunk and in a prescribed stupor from the night before. I was nothing but a body, running on autopilot fueled by toxic substances and hatred. I was a ghost of the person I once was and the potential that I once possessed. After months of physical therapy, I finally returned to work, but still suffered from chronic pain. Due to my injuries I could no longer work on the floor of the behavioral health hospital where I was employed. It was too much of a liability considering further injury on the job was highly probable, so I was given a position in Human Resources.

Despite my new administrative responsibilities, I continued the same lifestyle of severe substance dependence. There were times that I would come into work three hours late, no doubt reeking of alcohol. My approach about my behavior was shameless. I would walk into the

HR director's office and tell her, "I realize I am three hours late. I am not going to feed you some line of bullshit nor do I have a legitimate excuse. I'll be in my office when you are ready for me to sign that disciplinary action." Surprisingly, I was never written up and I was never fired. I eventually quit because it was nearly impossible to get out of bed and face the world sober.

In the state of decompensation that I was experiencing, my depression and trauma were too much to bear. I couldn't face the world sober for extended periods of time. I still managed to take some classes at the community college, but mainly because I was able to sneak off campus and self-medicate with marijuana and was constantly numb from the prescription pills. As soon as I left school, I either was hiding from the world in my bedroom or drowning out the world at a bar. I supported myself with taking out student loans and whatever money that I had been able to save from working. Eventually, even that light of a load became too much to bear. I failed out of college again and spent my days in a deep depression in my room. I just couldn't face the world and I couldn't face myself.

Something told me that I needed a dog to care for. I guess a part of me knew that I would eventually be able to learn to love, but I was incapable of learning through just caring for myself, so a dog seemed like a good idea. Every weekend I went to the Humane Society to search for that special dog. A couple of months went by, repeating this weekly ritual. Then one weekend, there she was. I knew it instantly. She was a beautiful, fawn-colored pit bull with amber eyes. She had the sweetest look about her, and she was just overflowing with love. She was a rescue who had been severely abused, but she didn't let that stop her from loving, and that was exactly what I needed to learn. I took her home and finally had a reason to get out of bed every day and when I was so depressed that I just lay staring despondently at the wall, she would lay right there with me with her head on my chest, with those big amber eyes overflowing with love. She would gaze at my face as if she was searching for my soul. For some it may sound strange, but I fully credit this four-legged being for teaching me how to love. She gave me purpose in my life at a time when I felt the emptiest. Her name was Moet, but that didn't seem to fit, so she became Militia.

I reenrolled in classes at the college and became active in several movements including the We the People Foundation for Constitutional Education and volunteering on Ron Paul's Presidential campaign. At one of the events a friend of mine introduced me to a young man who had been in and out of my life for years. It was Cain, that heavily tattooed violent punk rocker with the tattoo of the skeleton hand on his hand and the dragon tattooed on his head. He had made previous appearances briefly while Landon and I had been together. Ironically, he had been placed in Landon's class, where he was attending school for a degree in massage therapy. Since at the time I worked in a tattoo shop and knew all of the heavily tattooed people in the area, Landon thought it would be a good idea to introduce us, thinking that I already knew him. He had left Florida shortly after our meeting when I was fourteen and he travelled the country. When he was attending school with Landon, he had just moved back from New Mexico. We all got together and went out for drinks. At one point in the conversation he had said something to the effect that knowing my soul, I would be right at home in New Mexico. At the time I really didn't think too much of that comment. For one thing, I didn't even know my soul, and for another, I didn't have a passport, nor did I speak Spanish fluently, so why would I want to go to New Mexico? That tells you how much I knew about the state.

Apparently, Cain had really turned his life around and according to his account had become a completely different person. He was attending school to become a doctor of Chinese medicine and acupuncture, something that I had recently become interested in myself, as I had just had my first few treatments. We started spending more time together and I was immediately swept off my feet. He would say the sweetest things, like that he couldn't stop dreaming about me and that even when he was washing dishes, he would see my face in the reflection of the plate he was washing. I completely fell for it. He was kicked out of the place in which he had been living and of course, as always, it wasn't his fault, he was being completely victimized by everyone else, so I let him move in with me where I was renting a room.

Our influence on each other was like fire and gasoline. It was dangerous, explosive, and deadly. Any discord in the relationship was immediately my fault. I couldn't see it at the time, but my closest friends saw it from a mile away. But I just kept buying into it and falling deeper and deeper into the trap. Only a month or so after we started dating, we were in a near-fatal motorcycle accident. We had been drinking at a bar in downtown Orlando. One of the last things I remember was us realizing that we had left our helmets at one of the bars where we had been drinking. It somehow became a heated discussion…I can't really call it an argument, but more of a persistent persecution. My next memory was the realization that we had been in a wreck. I knew that my arm must've been broken, that there was a Buell Thunderbolt 1200 pinning me to the ground, and that there was the sound of someone screaming repeatedly; a terrified, blood-curdling scream. I soon realized that I was the one who was screaming, and Cain was standing over me in a panicked state, yelling at me to shut up.

We both sustained head injuries, but my injuries were much less serious than Cain's. I walked away with a couple of hairline fractures in my wrist and elbow, some road rash, and a "slight concussion," which I later found out was a traumatic brain injury. But still, compared to the driver, I was in much better condition. Cain had ruptured and lacerated a couple of his internal organs and it was quite apparent by his immediate change in personality that his head trauma was far worse. The Jekyll-and-Hyde cycle continued from then on. Whatever self-control he had practiced over his deviant desires and behavior was gone and I went along as a willing participant, at times even begging him to keep me captive under his wicked control. I had finally found someone who would treat me just as badly I as I felt on the inside.

It became obvious in a short period of time that my head injury was much worse than I initially realized. I could no longer function in school. Words, numbers, and figures would literally float off the page. My head was spinning. I couldn't think. I would get lost and break down in tears. I was in a near constant state of panic. My thoughts were unorganized, and I felt like I was incapable of making sense. I had absolutely zero short-term memory, I felt constantly confused, as though my mind was blanketed in a heavy fog. I became unable to work due to my inability to perform the most basic of essential job duties. I didn't have insurance at the time to get proper medical care. Things went downhill fast...my housing options became limited when my rent check bounced. I had taken Cain on as my responsibility since the accident had been my "fault." In my mind I had to take care of him and it was my responsibility to help him get better.

We downsized our belongings to what would fit into the vehicle that he had decided we would travel in, a 1952 Dodge Meadowbrook. I still can't believe that we made it from Orlando, Florida to Santa Fe, New Mexico in that thing. I think the brakes and front suspension were bad. The 2000 Ford 350 engine was mounted in with fabricated wooden mounts. It was a Frankenstein beast of a car. I was twenty-five years old, finally leaving the only place I had lived, to seek a new start or at least create one hell of a road trip story to tell. The only things I was taking with me were my dog Militia, an Army duffel bag, and my laptop to write my memoirs. Our first stop was New Orleans, Louisiana...The Big Easy.

Since I was in better shape than Cain, I sought out work wherever I could – restaurants, bars, strip clubs. The first opportunity of work I was offered was at Déjà Vu. It was my first time working as a dancer, and I was terrible at the job. I just naturally don't have what it takes for that industry, but because we were on the road and desperate for money, I took the job anyway. I hated myself even more and would have to get a head start on getting drunk before going in for my shift. I was becoming the type of woman that I had always felt pity for. Somehow, I could never see myself as being capable of getting into that position, yet here I was, an extremely beautiful, intelligent young woman, allowing herself to be exploited and abused in a dysfunctional relationship. I knew better; I just didn't feel like I was *worth* better.

The first time Cain punched me in the face was in front a bar in the French Quarter. He had a friend who worked as a bartender and was serving him unlimited cups of Maker's Mark Whiskey, not the best remedy for the recent injuries he had incurred only a month or so before. As we walked past a bar with an open dance floor, he turned and pointed at a small group of women in their early forties and began laughing obnoxiously in his drunken and delirious state. When he stopped, I simply reminded him that he wasn't that far away from being that age himself. As if he had forgotten who he was or how old he was, as if I had just said the most disgusting insult, he turned and punched me square in my nose. Initially, I thought he had broken it. A police officer responded to the "disruption we were causing," he searched us and told us to keep it down. Earlier in the evening, Cain had given me the keys to the car with the plan that he would drink as much as he wanted, and I would be the designated driver. By the time we reached the car, where we were parked along the street catty-corner to the police station, he decided that he wanted the keys back and was willing to use force to get them. In an attempt to get him to stop beating me, I got in the car and locked the doors. In his mind I was stealing his car, so he punched in the window, dragged me out, threw me into the street, and then threw my dog into the street. The next thing I knew, after scrambling over to retrieve a terrified Militia, I was being helped up off the pavement by a small group of young black men, who were obviously involved in some kind of crime or gang activity made evident by one of them asking me if I wanted them to "cap him right here." I told them "no, just get me to a safe place."

Within seconds of Cain getting in the vehicle and pulling away, he was pulled over for a DUI, indicating that the police had been aware of the situation that was going on and made the decision not to intervene in the domestic violence portion of the event and chose only to enforce the DUI law. I was of course a little apprehensive about traveling in a car with four men I didn't know, but as I requested, they took me to the people's house where we were living (technically we lived in their shed). A few years earlier, I had taken a part-time job on nights and weekends to earn extra income as a bartender at a strip club in Orlando. There were always one or two women, sometimes more, who worked as dancers and would come in to work after being beaten by their boyfriends to raise the funds to bail them out. I had no sympathy for them. I thought they brought it upon themselves. I didn't have a sliver of compassion for their situation. In March of 2008, I found myself in that exact situation.

The people in who's shed we were living would not allow Cain to return there to live. They had invited me to stay, saying that they would assist me with a place until I was on my feet, but I made the decision to continue with Cain on the journey. The next stop was Santa Fe, New Mexico. The mountains were calling my Soul, although I had not yet become aware of what that call was.

When we arrived in Santa Fe, one of Cain's longtime friends had gotten us positions working for a "trustafarian," me working as a housekeeper and him working on the outdoor crew. The job site was a $5 million estate on five acres, located on the outskirts of historic downtown Santa Fe. The estate itself was being remodeled and the property was being given an update. I eventually became a personal assistant/assistant property manager. The job offered good pay, a lot of perks, and fun people to be around for the most part, but there were dark secrets that soon started surfacing. The man who owned the estate and two other homes in the neighborhood was an heir to a man who made his money in oil and his mother had been a politician. The heir himself was a pharmacology school drop-out, part-time phi-losopher, and a full-time crack cocaine addict. The longer I worked for him, the darker secrets I discovered.

Things would seem to start to come together but would just as quickly (or even faster) fall apart. It was a constant dance of one step forward, two steps back. My intimate relationship with Cain fol-lowed that same pattern...forward, back, back, forward, back, back. The small steps forward made me hold onto to the hope that that truly would be the last time he would lose his temper. In June of 2008, right after my 26TH birthday, I discovered that I was pregnant. I immediately shifted gears and decided that I had a purpose and that I needed to make radical changes in my life to take care of that baby. Deep down I had a fear of becoming like my Mother and I was determined not to let that happen. Cain was on board with the pregnancy. We had already begun telling our friends and family that we were expecting; we started planning for the future of our family, until one night he came home drunk and started hitting me. That's when he informed me that I would *not* be having the baby. I left him that night to live at my boss's girlfriend's house, one of the three houses he owned in the neighborhood. The stalking behavior started… constant phone calls and texting, Cain standing behind trees in the yard watching the house, sweet-talking and apologies, promises that he would never behave like that again. I eventually buckled. By that point, I was so far into the cycle of abuse that I had alienated myself from my friends, had no safe support system, and did not realize at the time that I had been completely re-traumatized. I went back to him and once he had me isolated from my limited support, the abuse resumed. His words bore into my mind like parasites, robbing me of any common sense or self-preservation that I had. He convinced me that if I didn't have an abortion, he would ensure that I had a miscarriage no matter what lengths he had to go to, and that if I left him again, he would eventually find me no matter what, and that my consequences for running would be even worse. The detail with which he explained what he was going to do to me and our unborn child left me no doubt that he was telling the truth. A man who had such violent, sick thoughts was surely just as capable of executing them. In fact, I vaguely remembered my Mom telling me that my father had said something similar to her while she was expecting me. The night before going to Albuquerque to have the abortion, we stayed at a hotel in Santa Fe, where I let him inject Oxycontin into my arms while he told me that I was making the best decision because I was going to end up just like my Mother anyway. I wept and vomited over and over again throughout the night.

The next day he took me to the clinic while berating me the entire trip. At one point his words became so painful I attempted jumping out of the vehicle as it went full speed, southbound on Interstate 25. He swerved to keep me in the car. He promised me that as soon as I had the abortion, he would leave me alone, that we would be done. In the pre-counseling session I disclosed that I didn't want to do it, that I was being coerced into it, speaking I'm sure incoherently, at times sobbing, talking about her name, saying that I had already told my Grandmother and started buying clothes. The clinic staff asked me if they should call the police. I was scared out of my mind. I begged them not to, that Cain was in the waiting room, and that he would kill me if they did – even if he got arrested, he would eventually find me and kill me. We proceeded with the abortion. It was the most horrific experience of my life. It's something I said I would never do. I was the type who believed that in the right to a woman's choice, but I never imagined myself personally making that choice. As I wept on that table, begging for more sedation in between my sobs, I had the four-month-old embryo of my child; a piece of my very Soul, violently ripped from my uterus. I hated myself now, more than I ever thought possible.

Cain kept his promise and left for California, but not before trying to apologize and smooth over the damage in our relationship. But I stood firm in my rage and hatred. I got myself a vehicle and a small casita by myself out in a small orchard town in Northern New Mexico. I still worked for the same employer and now that I was on my own, became closer and closer to them (the "trustafarian," his girlfriend, and her daughters and granddaughter). This is when the dark secrets really began to surface. It turns out that when the girl-friend first started dating the millionaire, she looked the other way as he got one of her teenage daughters hooked on crack cocaine and sexually exploited her. By this time, I was so tormented, I was drinking with a death wish and had begun snorting cocaine with my boss. I didn't realize it at the time, but I believe that he was slowly conditioning me to be like the many women he exploited that worked for him or were in his company. It was obvious to me that I was on the verge of killing myself by the way I was using. I called the only person that I thought could help me; Cain.

I flew him back from California and it was like he never left, only now I was much more destructive and filled with more anger and rage than ever before. The domestic violence escalated to the point that we became a hazard to our own safety and the public's. We were totally out of control, but it was a familiar chaos that felt safer than what seemed like my only other option. The last night I drank, I decided that I just absolutely could not live like this anymore. In the middle of one of our fights on the side of the highway, I decided to throw myself in front of a car that was going at least 60 mph on a rural highway. The car swerved and missed me. Cain tackled me, knocking me out of the highway, and proceeded to hit me, then drag me across the highway by my hair to the car. He then knocked me out and threw me in the backseat. As he was driving my boss's SUV back to the casita where I lived, I came to, bewildered, not knowing where I was, who was driving, or where I was being taken. In a trauma-driven panic, I began kicking as hard as I could. I kicked Cain in the head, which resulted in his losing consciousness. He hit a tree and I flew forward, my head hitting the dashboard, resulting in my losing consciousness again.

When I came to, I again had no immediate recollection of what events had transpired. All I knew is that I smelled gunpowder and there were deployed airbags, so I deduced that I must be in a totaled vehicle. After taking a minute to gather my bearings, I got out of the vehicle and realized it was my boss's vehicle that I had been in. I went inside the casita to find Cain playing Xbox 360. I asked him what happened. He proceeded to tell me that I was the most fucked up person that he had ever met, that he was leaving tomorrow, and that he regretted ever coming back. As he continued to berate me, I went to the closet for the Glock 40, but being as drunk as I was, I fumbled with the pistol lock long enough for him to realize what I was doing. He came over and tried to take the gun away from me. The struggle resulted in my hitting myself in the face with the gun, and him taking it when I was stunned. I was still completely hell bent on total self-destruction, so I went to the kitchen and began drinking all of the chemicals under the kitchen sink. Within seconds, I fell, convulsing and vomiting blood. He came into the kitchen in a rage, screaming about how I should have waited until he left and kicking me in the stomach and the ribs as hard as he could. My landlord must have been unable to ignore the chaos any longer. Soon the New Mexico State Police and an ambulance arrived.

Part 2

The Insight Inside

"The unexamined life is not worth living"
- Socrates

5

Accepting the Medicine We Carry

"Through Love all that is bitter will become sweet
Through Love all that is copper will become gold
Through Love all dregs will become wine,
Through Love all pain will turn into Medicine."

\- Rumi

NOW IS AN opportune time for a brief interlude. I feel that it is necessary to give you some background on when, or should I say how my healing journey first began. I have always been bothered by the term *"shaman."* In fact, there was a period in my life that I was cynical and absolutely abhorred anything to do with the metaphysical, yet at the same time was strangely intrigued by the whole topic. My violent opposition to the idea of *shamanism* itself came from fraudulent people that I had met parading under that title. Essentially, however, a shaman/medicine is person is one who is familiar with realities other than the three-dimensional reality that we are aware of in our waking consciousness, one who work in many dimensions with the intent of healing others. A shaman/healer is one who is capable navigating the unseen world, seeing through the darkness and hearing answers in the silence. Although the details vary in each lineage, that common thread remains the same throughout cultures.

At a young age I was always fascinated by the idea of the shaman, medicine man/woman, healer, seer, the mystic, the witch etc. From a young age, I was painfully aware of more than what could be picked up by the average person's five senses. I had countless encounters with the supernatural as a child, so many that I went to my Grandmother and often spoke to her about them, as she seemed to be the only one who heard me and took me seriously. I would tell her about my dreams that served as premonitions, gut feelings that I would have that ended up being right, my ability to hear the needs of animals, how I could feel emotions that other people were feeling, or my ability to know when someone was in pain. She told me I had the family gift, that her Mother had had it as well. She shared with me her books by Black Elk, Edward Cayce, Vine Deloria Jr. and Nostradamus She taught me how to read tarot, view in her crystal ball, and use a pendulum. She told me that these gifts came from my Wazazi (Osage) lineage, as the people that resembled more closely the European lineage of the family seemed not to share these gifts. Aside from these things, I began my conversations with Creator at a young age. I felt most at home in the ritual of Mass at the Catholic parish where I attended school. Starting at the age of three, whenever I saw a phone booth, I would run to it, close the door, pick up the phone, and talk to Creator. I really don't have any recollection of these conversations. I vaguely remember the obsession with phone booths, but my Mom took countless photos of me doing this and my Osage Grandmother and Mother both attested to my doing that. While looking at those photos, I often wonder what I talked to Creator about at such a young age...and if I was actually listening to somebody else talk on the other end of the phone.

As a preteen, I began to explore paganism and witchcraft, a popular practice among many young girls, which is readily available and accessible in cities. I am unsure of whether it was my increasing interest in the dark arts that began exposing me to more negativity and trauma, or if my experience of more negativity and trauma drove my interest further into the dark arts and caused me to attract more people involved in such things. Whatever the case, the one thing I am sure of is that exposure to energies that are not understood can be extremely dangerous and lead one to one being vulnerable to demonic influence or possession. There were certain things that I witnessed and experienced as a young teen that have absolutely no logical explanation, most of which occurred directly before the darkest events of my life, I believe that that influence had been with my family for many generations. I was not the only person in my family that firmly believed that we were cursed. The Bible even speaks of this certain type of evil that comes in the form of generational curses, initially being mentioned in the Old Testament, specifically Deuteronomy 27 and 28, where incest, bestiality, and other sins are promised to be cursed, and mentioned again several times throughout the entirety of the document, citing many who were punished for the iniquities of their fathers. Whether demonic influence is sponsored by an entity known as the Devil or simply a byproduct of the dark side of the psyche that is contained within us all, I cannot say. What I do know is that living in denial that these dark energies have no influence over our everyday existence is an extremely dangerous position to take, as it leaves you vulnerable to being sideswiped by whatever that destructive force is.

After the darkest years of my youth, I had another powerful spiritual experience. It was directly after my first stay in treatment. I was still in an outpatient treatment program but was actively using for recreation. One week I had gotten some LSD from another one of the kids attending treatment. My friend Jessica and I decided to take it together during a sleepover. I got this idea that it would be funny if I pretended to be asleep for an extended period of time so that I could observe her and any peculiar behavior she exhibited under the influence. As I listened to her talk to herself and write in her journal, I was mimicking a breathing pattern that indicated that I was in deep sleep, unwittingly using yogic breathing to put myself in an altered state of consciousness, even more altered than that of the influence of the

LSD. In this state, I fell into a deep, deep, slumber in which I had the wildest dream. In my dream a medicine man sat across from me, a fire burning between us. He was clothed in some indigenous ceremonial garb, resembling that of some South American tribe. He spoke a language that I did not consciously understand, yet I understood the message of what he was saying to me. He threw a substance into the fire that made the fire flash, and within the fire I saw the vision of the warning he had been giving me. At that point I startled awake to find myself alone in my bedroom.

> "The perspective of trauma as an initiation is not a new one. Shamans in so-called primitive cultures all around the world have been initiated into the sacred and have discovered their visionary and healing powers through some kind of profound crisis, the common ones being near-death experiences, severe illness, schizophrenia, or major trauma. This initiatory crisis of the shaman is considered a religious experience in which the shaman is singled out by the Divine, marked as being different or other by the particularities of the trauma, and catapulted out of the world of ordinary reality into the territory of death and rebirth, the heart of the mystery of creation itself."[5]

The next day I went along with my day as usual and went into work. I had a job at the time at a restaurant in the neighborhood. I was out on a cigarette break sitting on a bench behind the restaurant. Seemingly from out of nowhere, a darker skinned man, short in stature, walked past me. I knew that I had seen him before, but I could not place from where I knew him. As soon as he walked into the restaurant he immediately walked out, having gotten nothing but a handful of napkins. He walked backward past me and said something in a language I didn't understand. I replied "excuse me." He turned around, still walking backward, and said, "I told you everything in the dream last night. It is imperative that you change your ways. Remember..."

---

5   "Trauma as Initiation: A Shamanic Perspective on Sexual Abuse" Suzanne Chassay

and walked away. I immediately felt chills in my spine. At first, I doubted my experience and rationalized it by the fact that I must still be under the influence, but despite my efforts to convince myself otherwise, I knew that I had seen him on the other side and that he had seen me, and that the message he had given me was a crucial one.

The next major episode happened roughly about seven years later when I was about twenty-two years old. I worked three jobs on the same street in downtown Orlando. I was a restaurant manager/bartender, a retail manager, and a body piercer/counter girl, all within the same city block. The retail store was called Kathmandu. The store sold all sorts of interesting imports from India and Bali. We stayed open until 3 a.m. on the weekends to accommodate the droves of drunk bar- and club-goers that wandered around the streets after last call. Once in a while somebody would make a late-night purchase. One such weekend, around 10 p.m. or so, a beggar wandered into the shop, but he wasn't your average homeless Floridian; in fact, he looked like he had just walked in off the streets of Calcutta. I asked him what I could do for him. He wanted to read my palm. I told him I had no money. He replied that he didn't want money, but rather a rudraksha seed necklace in return. I had no idea what the importance of that seed was in his culture or why he wanted it, but I continually declined his offer. He was adamant, however, about reading my palm. His reading was incredibly accurate. He knew things about my life that would be impossible to know. Toward the end of the reading he emphasized that I was going to die at a young age if I didn't change my path. Then he said something that made no sense at the time. He foretold of a time when I would finally find my home and when I came to this place I would know it because there would be many, many things that had been made with horseshoes. I was intrigued by his prediction. I began to rattle off questions about this home. All he would respond with was, "you will know." I told the shop owner about what had happened and asked him who the man was. He told me that they were Sikhs, the beggars and mystics of India, which I now know was total misinformation, but because of that misinformation I was introduced to Sikhism and ended up studying the religion more in depth in a world religions course that I was taking at the college.

Shortly after that incident, I began to have a desire to do something that made the world a better place. I wanted to give more in my own life that would lessen the suffering of others. I just didn't know what or how. One weekend working late at night, I was sexually assaulted at the shop by a drunk customer. I and the other staff who were working asked the man to leave the store. The owner of the shop was outside visiting with friends on the sidewalk and had noticed that there was some kind of incident. We explained to him what had happened, and he apologized to the customer and invited him back into the store, lecturing me that he was a paying customer. Infuriated, I went to the back and got my personal effects. On my way out, I told the business owner that if he wanted to pimp somebody out, it was going to have to be his own wife or daughter; it wasn't going to be me. I threw the shop keys at him and left. Weeks of bad luck seemed to swirl around this one event. The restaurant I worked at went out of business, a tattoo artist the shop where I worked died in a motorcycle accident, and an employee at the sub shop next door to Kathmandu left the oven on and burnt the building to the ground. After all these events transpired, I pursued work that was more meaningful. I started applying at different agencies to work with the less fortunate. In the interim, I took a job at a local health food store, at the time knowing nearly nothing about good health.

Working at the health food store was quite an experience of subculture shock after having had become accustomed to the environment that bars and tattoo shops afforded. At the time I still ate an atrocious diet and had little-to-no self-care skills. I half-jokingly described myself as being "feral." For some reason, however, I had always had an interest in the Eastern cultures, most likely because of my Uncle's influence. He had lived in Thailand for years after the Vietnam War and became skilled in martial arts. With this piqued curiosity, I also was interested in drinking tea. The first tea that I ever bought was Yogi Tea. For some reason there was no question about what brand kind or brand of tea I would get; it was if I had already known and just remembered. I was fascinated with this tea brand. I wondered if the man with the turban and beard on the side of the box was real. I would sit and read the tea tabs and ask this image questions. This image turned out to be Yogi Bhajan, a man who I would know well, but I wouldn't know for several years.

My experience of working in the health food store ended very quickly after witnessing a girl get her finger mutilated in a wheatgrass juicer. From that job I began my ten-year career in the behavioral health field in varying capacities. I began my career in the field of Applied Behavioral Analysis, the science of behavior that is measured from that which is observable and measurable. It was very objective, dry, predictable, with formulas...it was in fact a hard science. I got to do some very meaningful work with autistic children and adults. One day while I was at the bookstore buying books by B.F. Skinner & John B. Watson, a book called *Synchronicity: An Acausal Connecting Principle* by C.G. Jung all but jumped out off the shelf in front of me. A co-worker thought it strange for someone who was taking a graduate course in the study of Applied Behavior Analysis to be reading that book simultaneously as if to indicate that it would be impossible to entertain the two incredibly different theories in one's mind at the same time. What Jung had to say about this theory made a lot of sense to me then, as it does today. When viewing life through the lens of connection it gives life more meaning, and one begins to see Creator everywhere. Despite how logical, practical, and mundane life became, I still had an affinity for the mystical.

For years I had lost touch with this essence of myself, but about a year after my motorcycle accident, when I quit drinking, I began to see instances of serendipity pulsing through my life again. And it is this essence that I feel played a large part in my own recovery and the soul retrieval work that I so enjoy today. In fact, I have become much more comfortable with the word "shaman," not that I ever had anything against traditional shamans, but I took more issue with the ideas the word conjures up in the Western mind, not to mention that you can now take online shamanism courses and earn a Ph.D. in said field. When I think of the word shaman now, it simply means one who is aware of the vibration of the Soul and can do the work in that realm. This culture is in dire need of more people who are willing to do this deeply committed spiritual work. It seems that the American culture has lost touch with its soul. So many people have become so empty, so numb, so despondent...my heart aches when I see this pain in people. For I know that pain all too well myself. Eventually I felt like my daily life was meaningless and task-driven, that I was ineffectual, consumed by fear, inferior to everyone around me. I was highly critical of myself and others, I was overweight, chronically ill, I protected my heart with walls of steel, and worst of all, I had for-gotten how to dream. There were many mornings that I woke up crunching numbers in my head, furious and anxiety ridden before my feet even hit the floor. I would continually seek to numb this feel-ing with prescription drugs, illicit drugs, alcohol, shopping, and sex. Nothing worked. I felt so disconnected – from myself, from others, and from Creator, from life itself.

I have realized on my journey of healing that I wasn't the only one feeling this way. American culture is plagued with this sense of emptiness and detachment. According to a BBC investigative report, Americans use 80% of the global supply of prescription pain killers. It's no secret that opiate addiction is now an epidemic in the United States as a result of this overprescribing. These figures don't even consider the over prescription of anti-depressants and benzodiazepines. Of course, there are times when needing medication is absolutely valid, however in most situations, it's a case of learning symptoms manage-ment or lifestyle changes. Often, psychotropic medications are offered to treat emotions associated with living life on life's terms, for instance a primary care physician will often offer an antidepressant to an indi-vidual experiencing the grief of losing a loved one. Life if meant to be experienced and felt. When we numb our capacity to feel pain, we also numb out our capacity to experience joy. This type of detachment cre-ates an anxiety and depression. Rather than seeking that connection that would catalyze emotional healing, the person is lead to believe that adding another medication will relieve the depression and anxiety associated with this type of detachment. The clinical name for soul loss is the split self, which is a fitting a name as it is the result of the soul splitting away from the body. From what I have learned this is incredibly common, especially with individuals who have been diagnosed with Post Traumatic Stress Disorder. It seems that whenever one is exposed to trauma or is forced to do things that a person in good conscience would never do (such as killing when at war), soul loss occurs. I have had teachers explain that when the Soul feels threatened it will, for lack of better terms, vacate the body in order to protect itself in its state of purity. This explanation fits perfectly into my understanding of the way in which we were created, as it says in the Christian story of creation as do many traditions around the world, "And God said, "Let us make man in our image, after our likeness..." surely we are not made in the physical likeness of Creator because Creator Itself is formless and omnipresent. Certainly, it cannot be that our mind was made in the image of Creator because the human mind, as vast as it is, has its limitations, so this essence in creation stories around the world must be referring to the fact that our Soul is the very part of us that is made in the likeness and image of Creator. Since Creator is pure consciousness and humans are beings that possess a consciousness that can perceive a power greater than itself, which is what sets us apart from other animals, then naturally one could conclude that a piece of Creator's consciousness is within us all; The Ultimate Observer. So, when one witnesses, experiences, or commits an act that is insulting to Creator; consciousness in its purest form, that part of us does what it needs to do to retain its state of purity. This shamanic explanation would account for why people who have been to war or experienced other traumatic circumstances report feeling as if they were vacant, a hollow shell of the person they once were. That's because a part of them has gone missing.

"In many shamanic societies, if you came to a medicine person complaining of being disheartened, dispirited, or depressed, they would ask one of four questions. When did you stop dancing? When did you stop singing? When did you stop being enchanted by stories? When did you stop finding comfort in the sweet territory of silence?" From Gabrielle Roth

Sadly, allopathic medicine has no framework for diagnosing soul loss in Western culture, but the symptoms are seen daily by physicians across the United States. These symptoms manifest as chronic aches and pains, depression, anxiety, weight gain, and insomnia. Often times these symptoms are simply misdiagnosed as a mental illness and medications are prescribed to mask the symptoms. But these are merely a Band-Aid. Without the cause truly being addressed, the wound begins to fester and the infection persists.

Luckily, there are many ways to retrieve one's Soul. I am living proof. Once I had finally quit drinking and made the declaration that I was going to heal, Creator began supporting this intention by placing many amazing healers in my life. On such person was Dr. Harijot, an 80-year-old blind Shen Acupuncturist. I will never forget my first visit. Upon taking my pulse for diagnosis, he gave me a perplexed look. He said, "You were writing a book of some kind, like a personal memoir. Why did you stop?" I explained to him that my boyfriend at the time had smashed my laptop in one of his fits of rage. His response to me was, "you need to finish writing that book." I became certain in that moment that telling my story was in the design of my Soul, the blueprint that Creator had given for my life.

"The true wisdom of a shaman is learned through suffering and isolation. The experience of crisis or trauma takes her out into the solitary wilderness where she must confront the unspeakable alone with no maps or reference points to guide her. In this place there is nothing but raw experience itself, pristine and shattering. She is severed from her personal and cultural history and literally hurled into the abyss of unknowing. Trauma thus becomes the catalyst that enables her to break the veils of ordinary reality and social norms and forces her to confront alone that which she most fears so that her spirit is widened to encompass the cosmos itself and the universal ground of being.

On her return she has become the healed healer who has been able to retrieve the fractured shards of body and psyche and integrated the seemingly irreconcilable planes of life experience: the ordinary and the sacred, the mythic and the historic, male and female, light and dark, life and death. Thus, she becomes the master of thresholds, able to hold and work with the balance of opposites, the paradox of divine reality that is woven into the unitary tapestry of splendor and brutality that is at the very heart of life and what it means to be human. Her quest is to know the sacred, she welcomes the initiation of trauma, recognizing it as a gateway. Her efforts to embrace paradox involve her in a process of constant transformation. Creating a fluidity between shifting states of consciousness that lays bare the essence of that which does not change: pure awareness, the luminosity of Being itself.

The focus of shamanic initiation is to enter the mystery by becoming it, to transcend death by dying into life, to pierce reality by embracing opposites and to reunite the fractured worlds of sickness and health, life and death, so that their oneness and interconnection can be revealed."[6]

---

6   "Trauma as Initiation: A Shamanic Perspective on Sexual Abuse" Suzanne Chassay

6

Kundalini Rising

"Kundalini yoga presented Jung with a model of something that was almost completely lacking in Western psychology--an account of the development phases of higher consciousness.... Jung's insistence on the psychogenic and symbolic significance of such states is even more timely now than then."
- The Psychology of Kundalini Yoga by
C.G. Jung, Sonu Shamdasani

As I WAS being rushed to the hospital in Española, New Mexico, the death by opiate overdose (per capita) capital of the United States,[7] the paramedics asked who had beaten me, asking if it was my boyfriend. As a knee-jerk reaction, I lied. I said that I had hit my face on the counter when I collapsed. How ridiculous that lie seems now, because to cause that kind of damage to myself, I would have had to repeatedly smash my head on the counter and found a creative way to crack my own ribs. But that is the paradox of an abusive relationship. The victim

---

7   United States Department of Justice www.justice.gov

for some reason feels obligated to protect their offender. I don't remember too much else, aside from the fact that a nurse came in and told me that she had never seen anything like this before.

The last chemical I drank somehow neutralized all of the other chemicals, so it wouldn't be necessary to pump my stomach or give me charcoal. She made a comment about how blessed I was. Needless to say, I was not in the most graceful of spaces at the time and I responded crassly, "Fuck you. You obviously don't know what I was trying to do." She looked at me in dismay and continued adjusting my IV, telling me that I was going to be kept for observation overnight for the esophageal burn, which came as a surprise, as I was expecting to be held in a psychiatric unit for my suicidal behavior.

"Never lose hope, my heart, miracles dwell in the invisible."

- Rumi

The next day Cain showed up at the hospital to berate me and tell me what a terrible human being I was. I broke down in tears. I just couldn't do it anymore, I couldn't pretend to be okay. I had lost my ability to smile and say that I was alright. I couldn't keep up the façade anymore. I still wanted to die, but it became obvious from the events of the night before that Creator wasn't going to let me go anywhere. Creator had a purpose for me and there was a part of the contract that I still had yet to fulfill. I had absolutely no idea how to live and I realized that at that moment in that hospital bed. As if my unspoken prayer had been heard, Cain got up and said, "I'm going to the nurse's station to find someone to talk to you." As if being divinely guided, he asked the perfect person to come talk to me. She asked him to leave the room. I don't remember the exact words of that conversation, but I do remember clearly what the conversation felt like. Her name was Laurel and she was a recovering addict. She looked at me through the eyes of someone who had personally known that all-consuming self-hatred. Not once did she say, "What's wrong with you?" For the first time I felt like I was being seen for what was *right* with me.

*"I have learned that people will forget what you
said, people will forget what you did, but people will
never forget the way that you made them feel."*
- Maya Angelou

During the course of our conversation, Laurel brought up going to Twelve-Step meetings. Of course, I had every rebuttal in the book. Not once did she lose her temper, nor did she walk away throwing her hands in the air because I was too much. She stayed and had a compassionate answer to everything I said. That day was November 21, 2008. I was in an AA meeting on 23rd to pick up my first 24-hour chip in eight years. Somehow, I had survived my own attempt at self-destruction, and it was certainly due to no effort of mine. I like to joke and say that I was Creator's personal trainer, because I certainly made Her run after me.

Before I left the hospital, Laurel gave me her Narcotics Anonymous card and the phone number of a man who lived up the road from me who would most likely give me rides to meetings. Never in my life would I have called a stranger to pick me up and take me anywhere, let alone a meeting, but I had been blessed with the gift of desperation. That was the week of the NA area Thanksgiving feast. "Free" and "food" have always been two of my favorite words in the English language, so I went. My expectations were certainly exceeded when I left with more than just a full belly. Apparently, my heart had been cracked open, and while I sat and listened to people share their gratitude for how their lives had transformed, hope seeped into that crack and filled my heart. I left with the hope in knowing that there was another option, that people who had reached the low depths in life that I had, had found a way to live and to do so happily. So, I kept going.

Life seemed to accelerate immediately. It felt unfair, because I didn't know how to handle anything sober. I went to as many meetings as I could. Simply knowing that it would be impossible for me to use during that hour came as a huge relief. The support and love from fellow NA members was tremendous. Shortly after getting sober, I got a call from my Mom. My Grandmother was in hospice and was asking for me to come home. This was something I had said I would never be able to handle, even when I was drinking. I loved my Grandmother dearly. I knew that I was going to need all the support I could get, so I prayed and prayed. The support came nearly immediately. My sponsor helped me figure out a plan, I met a Lakota elder that supported me through sweat lodge and ceremony, and somebody loaned me a copy of the *Tibetan Book of the Dead*. There was one more thing that I had to do before leaving, and that was enroll in one of the local universities.

I had my eye on St. John's College or possibly Highlands University. I had immediately ruled out the college in Española; it was, after all, the death by opiate overdose (per capita) capital of the United States,[8] so there was no way I was going to that school. As it turned out, I got lost driving into Santa Fe and ended up at the college in Española. Having such a deep belief in meaningful coincidences, I decided to humor God and see what She might have in store for me. Upon walking up to the registration table, my eye was immediately caught by a flyer that read: "Kundalini Yoga for Addiction Recovery, pilot program, Harvard Study." I had never heard of Kundalini Yoga before, but I had quit drinking about thirty days before that. I was desperate to try anything, since religion and the Twelve Steps alone wouldn't be enough to keep me sober. So, I enrolled at Northern New Mexico College in Española.

Interestingly, it is said that Bill W. was inspired to create Alcoholics Anonymous after a suggestion he received while he was in correspondence with Carl G. Jung. The famous Swiss psychoanalyst contended that once the spiritual malady had begun being addressed and the alcoholic realized there was a power greater than themselves functioning in the Universe, then that recovering alcoholic would as a result begin to experience frequent states of serendipity in their lives. These events, which could be written off as being coincidences, were in fact

---

8   United States Department of Justice www.justice.gov

Creator's way of remaining anonymous, while simultaneously giving one the necessary road signs to let the person know they were on the right path. The coincidence of my getting lost as a result of my head injury was certainly one of those road signs.

A day or so after enrolling in school I was on a flight to Florida. When I got to the hospice, I couldn't believe what my eyes were seeing. My Grandmother had wasted away to nearly nothing. She was covered in very large decubitus ulcers along her back. She was malnourished to the point of inertia. One of my uncles had disclosed to me that my Mom had been stealing the grocery money and using it for crack cocaine, supplementing whatever food she could get from neighbors and food pantries to feed my Grandmother and herself. My Mom had been finding receipts in parking lots to pass off to the executor of the estate for bookkeeping purposes. I was infuriated. How could they have done this? And there lay my once beautiful Grandmother, moaning in pain, barely holding onto to the life that she once knew. But even in my frantic state and scrambled mind, I knew this wasn't about them; this was about her.

For the next four days I lived at that hospice. I had the nurses wheel in a bed and I slept there by my Grandmother. It was the first week in January 2009. She would fade in and out of consciousness, sometimes totally lucid and other times talking to her Daddy, who had been deceased since she was a young girl. We watched the inauguration together and sang the National Anthem together. She expressed gratitude and her astonishment that she had lived long enough to see the first black president elected. She joked with me and said that now I had a better chance of becoming the first woman president, a dream I'd had in my childhood. I brushed and braided her hair and I listened. I listened to whatever last pieces of wisdom she was willing to share. As the days went by she became less and less lucid. I called the priest to deliver her Last Rites, as she was a devoted Catholic. The process of dying was so accurately outlined in the *Tibetan Book of the Dead*, it appears as though they had it process of death down to a science. As she reached the next stage in the process, I would read to her the coordinating passage and prayers, most of which simply reminded the Soul to not be tricked by the illusion and trappings of this world, that she had permission from all of those who loved her to go in peace, and that she could do so without fear because she was going home to her Father.

After she passed, the rage that I felt towards my Mother came flooding back and I wanted justice. I stormed out into the hall demanding to speak to the social worker. When she came to greet me, I immediately asked how I would go about pressing charges on her caregiver for neglect. I don't know how she did, but she convinced me to let it go, most likely because it would be very difficult to pursue pressing charges while in another in another state. So, I let go of the idea and caught a flight back home to New Mexico. I knew that if I had stayed for the funeral that I would not have been able to control my anger and my Mother would be on the receiving end, so I let go.

As it tends to do, life persisted upon my return. A day or two after I returned, the engine in my Ford Explorer blew. A week or so after that, I finally asked Cain to contribute to rent and a fight ensued. Rather than pay rent, his plan was to go buy a new motorcycle. The verbal altercation quickly escalated when he started punching me in the face. I froze; I couldn't fight back. I was curled in a fetal position protecting my face the best that I could as he continued to hit me repeatedly with his fist. In that moment I remembered a story that one of the yoga teachers had told in one of my first Kundalini Yoga classes. It was an anecdotal story of Ike and Tina Turner. One time when he was beating her, she started repeating a mantra that she had learned even though she had no idea what it meant. That moment was the beginning of the end of their relationship.

The week before in my weekly three-hour Kundalini Yoga class at the college, we covered a section on mantra and we were asked to choose a personal mantra, one that resonated with us. I chose a mantra that had the power to stop anything negative, one that was so powerful that it would put the mind in reverse, remove any and all obstacles, and bring the practitioner great intuition. For some reason in that moment when Cain was beating me, I thought of that and began reciting the mantra and recited it. Within seconds my neighbor was at the door yelling that she was calling the police. Cain ceased the attack and continued packing his car to make his escape. My neighbor took me into her home and we called the police. For the first time in my life, I felt heard by law enforcement. They took the report along with photos of my injuries. I filed an Order of Protection through the Santa Fe courts and was granted an order lasting for 105 years. I learned quickly, however, that this process is painfully re-traumatizing. First, you must know where the person against whom you are trying to get an order lives, works, or frequents. Then you must pay a process server a certain amount of money to serve them their papers. If the server cannot reach them after two attempts, you are out of your money. Allegedly this process server encouraged Cain to file for an Order of Protection against *me* and offered him a discount on serving his papers to me.

If you are successful in having the court order served, then you must go sit in court and face your offender and sit through having your character completely thrashed. I sat through the court proceedings as he brought up my juvenile record and my two arrests in Florida for aggravated assault and battery. That I could handle, because it was true, but then he went into morbid details of how I would abuse him and that I had run off and aborted his child as an attempt to manipulate and hurt him. I nearly vomited on the courtroom floor. I was so blessed to have had my NA sponsor there at the time; otherwise I think I may have truly lost myself and reacted to the trap he was attempting to set. After his dramatic testimony, the judge made it very clear to him that despite his story, the evidence concluded that he was the primary aggressor, and I was granted the Order of Protection.

I assumed from the language used in the paperwork and court proceedings that this meant that I was protected. One of the mandates of the order was that he could not be in possession of any firearms while this order was in effect. I called the police several times in an effort to verify that he had surrendered his firearm. He had not. Within weeks he began violating the order by showing up at the same meetings that

I was attending. The order clearly stated that if he showed up to a location that I was already at, he would need to leave; however, if I showed up at a location where he was, then it would be the socially polite thing for me to leave. He would show up, sit across the room, and glare at me. I had called the police on one or two occasions, but they never showed. If they did, it was long after I left. I called the police station repeatedly to let them know that he was in violation of the order by still possessing firearms. They said there was nothing that they could do, that he would have to have his firearm on him while violating the Protection Order for them to be able to pick him up. Otherwise, it was up to him to use his "good judgment" to surrender his firearm. The law expected a self-identified sociopath, who had previously tried to kill me, to use his "good judgment" and cooperate with a piece of paper a judge had signed; otherwise, the only way they could intercept was if he had his firearm on him while he was stalking me. Learning from the history of the New Mexico law enforcement, by the time they responded to that call, not if, but *when* it happened, I would have been dead. I realized that I really wasn't protected after all.

I was attending my weekly Kundalini Yoga class and this specific week was going to be my first experience of ever doing a gong meditation. The gong is an ancient and powerful instrument of transformation that is unique to eastern practices. It is a symphonic gong that is played while the listener lays in Shavasana (corpse pose) or a seated meditative posture. The powerful sound and vibratory frequency powerfully synergizes within the listener, bringing that person into a state of harmony on a cellular level. As I began to drift off in meditation, I began to see images in my mind. My life, my Mother's life, my Grandmother's life, and my Great-Grandmother's life all flashed through my mind in what seemed like seconds. It was as though I had opened a 3- D, pop-up book in my mind and patterns began emerged. I realized the words that Cain had said to me while I was pregnant were nearly identical to the words my Father had said to my Mother when she was pregnant with me, at least according to my Mother's account. "If you run and have that baby, I will kill you *and* the baby."

How often did I tell Cain that he reminded me of my Grandfather? Too many times. And the way he financially exploited me was so similar to the way I had been exploited before. I was starting to see a pattern, a pattern that I was not only repeating in my own life but that had been repeated by every woman on the maternal side of my family. I also realized that the man who had brought Kundalini Yoga to the United States in 1969 was none other than Yogi Bhajan, the man on the Yogi Tea box that I had started my silent conversations with years before.

It was in those quiet moments out on those acres in that small orchard town, when I was by myself, that I felt the craziest. There was no one to argue with, no one to tell me I was worthless. There was no drama, no fighting, no drinking, no drugging. There was only me and my thoughts. I wanted to rip my skin off and run away. I would pace and pace, just itching to break something to create some sort of drama, something to break that awful silence that was deafening to my ears and painful to my heart. I would go on hikes either by myself or with my trusted four-legged friend Militia. My emotions were so backed up. My thoughts were a swirl of grief, anger, gratitude, and more anger. My memory was still terrible, as a result of the multiple head injuries and years of drug and alcohol abuse. Aside from the mantra there was only one other practice I had learned in the yoga class that I could recall at will and that was *Sat Kriya*. Out in the foothills of Northern New Mexico, I would drop to my knees and assume that posture and chant for as long as I could, which wasn't long at all, and each time I did this practice, I would break down in tears collapsing in the dirt, sand, and rocks of those hills. I didn't know what was happening, but something was shifting within me. The wall of tears began to fall. Soon I began crying every day, sometimes multiple times a day, and they weren't always tears of sadness or loss. Often, they were tears evoked by a beautiful sunset, song lyrics, or a touching share at a Twelve-Step meeting. I finally figured out what was happening to me. I was beginning to feel, sometimes so deeply that I wondered how I had lived my life for so long in a state of numbness.

By this time, I had gotten back with Cain. We moved into a tiny place in the Santa Fe National Forest in a small community by the ski basin. I knew that this was not the best choice, but with the little support I had received from the "justice" system, my options were limited. The house I was renting was the tack house for the ranch. It was perfect for one person and a stretch for two people who got along well. There was a cabinet above the kitchen sink...well, it looked like a cabinet. It was actually a vent for the bathroom, so this little wooden door opened, and you could see directly into the bathroom from the kitchen. Often, I would lock myself in the bathroom to get away from the verbal assaults and Cain would walk right around to the kitchen, open the cabinet, and continue on with his monologue. Luckily the land we were on was beautiful and I found my sweet escape in nature. Being in the national forest, there was a plethora of wildlife. Bears and mountain lions would literally come to our front door, but I felt safer with them than I did with Cain, most likely because they were more predictable. I spent a lot of my time reading in a hammock I had hung up alongside the stream, while Militia ran about and played in the water. I learned a lot about meditation in those woods. I knew that I was getting somewhere when I had several encounters where doe and coyotes would come close to my vicinity while I was sitting in meditation.

In November of 2009 I took a third-shift job working at a homeless shelter while I attended school. The extreme schedule did something to my brain. I started experiencing some familiar symptoms that I recognized as a result of sleep deprivation when I was younger. What I didn't know yet is that I was finally beginning to experience the symptoms of Post-Traumatic Stress Disorder that I had so artfully learned to self-medicate with alcohol and benzodiazepines. At this point, I had been sober for nearly a year now, and my symptoms were perpetually getting worse. When I did sleep I had horrific nightmares. I was often "zoned out," which I now know is called dissociation. I would often be confused as to what day or time it was, and I was having more and more difficulty completing basic daily activities.

When my symptoms became too much to bear, I finally went and sought help from a local behavioral health agency. The man who did my assessment suggested that I see one of their therapists. I had my first unofficial appointment with Lynn. Immediately she reminded me of my Mother – the fair skin, bright eyes, and beautiful red hair. She reminded me of the beautiful attributes that my Mom once possessed before her addiction robbed her of them. I told Lynn as much about my life as I was comfortable disclosing. After the brief interview, she said it would probably be best if I worked with a therapist trained in Eye Movement Desensitization and Reprocessing (EMDR) therapy, but that she would love it if I came over to see the advocacy café that she ran. This was the first time I was officially diagnosed with PTSD.

I started volunteering at Sojourners Advocacy Café and attending therapy. Eventually I was prescribed a substance that really helped my symptoms (medical cannabis), and my symptoms once again became manageable. This seemed like nothing short of a miracle because throughout the most difficult times, sometimes so difficult that I thought I would be stuck in a permanent state of trauma induced psychosis, I continued my Kundalini Yoga practice, although it may have only been a three-minute breathing exercise every day I knew that that three minutes was having a profound effect on me. I continued on in school and eventually completed my degree in substance abuse counseling. Upon getting my addictions counseling license, I was offered full-time employment at the behavioral health agency that funded Sojourners Advocacy Café. Around the same time that agency became the first and only agency in the state that took referrals for victims of human trafficking. When I began working with these young women, I felt a compassion that I had never felt before. When I began to learn what human trafficking was, I started to realize that the same thing had happened to me. I was finally able to see myself as a victim of a crime rather than just a "drug-addicted teenage prostitute", as I was told I was, who made bad decisions. For the first time I began to experience a sense of compassion for myself and my past through the compassion I felt for these other young women.

It was by this time that I had gained an awareness of what was influencing my emotional states. Previously I had only been aware of bad moods and assumed naturally that they were being caused by outside influences, but slowly I started to listen to my own thoughts. I would catch myself glancing in the rearview mirror and realize that I was thinking how ugly I was or that I was worthless. I began to be more and more mindful of this and when I would catch myself, I would stop the thought and plug in a new incompatible thought, something that I loved about myself. At that time there really wasn't anything that I liked about myself except for my eyes. I've always liked my eyes, within in them I always saw reflected a deep longing for connection. So, when I would catch myself spewing self-loathing thoughts in my head, I would stop, connect with myself in the mirror, and tell myself I had beautiful eyes. The more aware that I became of my thoughts and my reactions to external situations, the more I was able to change the essential patterns of my thinking, conditioning myself to think more loving thoughts.

As a result of my yoga and meditation practice growing, I continued to grow as well. I had graduated Magna Cum Laude, had an amazing mentor at work, and was continually promoted. I enrolled in a bachelor's program integrating psychology, humanities, and Pueblo Indian studies. I was experiencing such rapid healing from my yoga practice that I wanted to share it with others.

There was a woman at the agency whom everyone had given up on. Her mental and physical health had deteriorated so much I think that all of her providers had lost hope. In fact, one of her doctors had told her that she just needed to check into a long-term care facility and wait for her organs to continue failing until she expired. She had asked to be transferred to my caseload, which of course I obliged. At the time she could barely leave her home, so I would meet her at her apartment once or twice a week and work on case management, co-ordination of care, showing her Kundalini practices. I knew that her Soul wasn't ready to leave yet despite the extent of damage that her brain and body had suffered. I knew from personal experience that once you integrate the Soul, reconnecting to your Divine propose, all other healing that the body and mind need will follow. When I refer to integrating one's soul into their healing goals, I am referring to the process of Soul retrieval and through this process an individual awakens to the fact that they are more than their mind and their body, they are their Soul and that is what is at the very core of an individual's existence. It is the process of recognizing the part of ourselves that was made in the image of the Creator. Through that connection, all healing is possible. So we did that work together every week in her living room. She began experiencing results immediately and insisted that I teach this practice to others. I set up a small class at the advocacy café and began integrating techniques into the groups that I ran. It was miraculous how impactful the technology of Kundalini was. It was as though it reminded the body that it already knew how to heal itself.

I consulted with one of my yoga teachers before starting the class, since at that point I was not yet a certified teacher. A month or so later, however, I started my Kundalini Yoga Teacher Training Course in Santa Fe. How impactful that nine-month training was! I learned more about myself in that short time than I had learned in my entire life. Yoga is a Sanskrit word that translates to the word yoke or union. My practice unified my mind, body, and spirit into a complete being, unified me with all of humanity, and above all, unified my complete being with Creator. And through this union I received deep insight into myself, others, the nature of life and death, and some of the most pressing issues in our world today.

7

Sins of the Father, Sins of the Mother

"Contrary to popular misconception, karma has nothing to do with punishment and reward. It exists as part of our holographic universe's binary or dualistic operating system only to teach us responsibility for our creations- and all things we experience are our creations."

- Sol Luckman

BEING THAT I had never met my father, had only seen his name on my birth certificates and heard a couple second-hand accounts from a few people, I always wondered if the thought of my existence ever crossed his mind. My Mother had pursued him for child support in the past, but I don't think the results were very successful. I recall hearing the words "dead-beat dad" while growing up. I really know very little about him except that he was Basque and Cherokee in ethnicity and originally from West Virginia. Allegedly he was a small-time criminal, an alcoholic, a womanizer, and he liked to get into bar fights.

Several years ago I decided to get an Ancestry account online to pursue my family's longtime goal of accumulating genealogy facts on our lineage. My Grandfather had purchased several books about his surname, but nothing had ever been done with the books. My first research was for records on my Father. I found his information in Florida and West Virginia. One such piece of information was a marriage license that indicated that he was married at the time of my conception. I can't say I was exactly shocked, but my Mother had never mentioned this detail. Maybe that is what she meant by saying that he was a womanizer. So many questions ensued...Did she know? Had he promised her that he would leave his wife? Was he leading a double life? These are questions that may forever go unanswered.

It wasn't until years later that I realized the full implications of what this meant. Since my family was Catholic and my Mother was having a child out of wedlock, that meant that I was her real-life "scarlet letter." I represented the shameful act of having sex out of marriage and getting caught, so it's no wonder her repressed emotions would come out and be directed at me. Could she have been conscious of her behavior and what was driving it? Most likely not, as most people lack insight into themselves, but it began to make total sense. Similarly, I was evidence of my Father's infidelity. And as my Mother had alleged, whenever she would pursue him for child support, he would call and threaten to kill me, so I could see where he would develop a motive for making such threats, being that he was already married with a family and the threat of exposing his infidelity, having a child out of wedlock while being married, jeopardized all of that. My mere existence threatened his entire way of life as he knew it. I am not condoning their behaviors and motives, but I can see what was driving their behavior; fear.

This realization had to sit with me for several months before I could fully feel it. In November 2013 I was driving back from my Thanksgiving vacation at a friend's ranch. As I was driving, I thought about the way in which these two people brought me into the world. Then, I suddenly, finally felt an incredibly deep heartache over not being wanted by my parents. I began to weep so hard, I had to pull off at an exit. I parked my car near a cotton field and wept. When I recomposed, I started journaling about how this had affected me throughout my life.

Epigenetic theory contends that environmental influences can have an effect on genes that causes certain codons to be switched on and off, essentially changing the genetic makeup of the being. These environmental influences can certainly include stress. And the science of quantum mechanics states that even emotional states can have a lasting effect on subatomic particles within the cell, again shaping the genetic makeup of the one being influenced. With that stated, imagine how abusive and highly stressful environments can negatively impact the developing fetus. The saying goes, "neurons that fire together, wire together".[9] If a fetus experiences everything that the Mother does during the pregnancy, then of course negative emotions will impact the developing child. The heart is the first organ to fully develop in the embryo; a heartbeat can be heard by the first 40 or so days of pregnancy. Keeping this in mind, my Mother alleges that my Father hit her while she was pregnant and that's when she left him. I assume that there is more to the story, because there always are two sides of any story, and somewhere in the middle lies the truth.

When all of this information began to converge in my mind, I concluded that I had been genetically altered to have little to absolutely no shame resistance. I had been consumed by shame since as long as I could remember. My very first memory at two years old includes the words, "shame on you." As I described earlier, as a child, whenever I was victimized, whether as a result of abuse or of being bullied, I always felt an immense sense of shame. Aside from the neurobiological predisposition for shame as a result of my Mother's situation while I was in utero, there is also the culture of shame that single mothers have experienced for millennia.

Growing up in a Catholic school and community, I realized at a very young age that the structure of my family was much different from every other family in the parish. All the other families were

---

9   1949 by Donald Hebb, Canadian neuropsychologist

nuclear in nature, but mine consisted of myself, my Mother, and my Grandparents. Although I was too young to catch all the cultural subtleties in communication, my Mother must have experienced some level of shaming in her interactions as well. My shame was mostly centered around not having a father. I remember thinking that there must have been something wrong with me or that I did something wrong that made him leave, that somehow, I was inferior to the other children because I was a bastard child.

It's interesting that the psychoanalytic field has studied the mother-daughter relationship so thoroughly that it has been determined that a poor relationship with one's mother could undoubtedly cause the development of borderline personality disorder. There has been an entire phenomenon labeled "The Mother Wound," but what of the father's transgressions and iniquities? It is widely known that the absence of a father is detrimental to the development of a child as well, so why is there no "Father Wound" emergent theory, and why are there not personality disorders that indicate an absent father as the cause? Well, our culture has been blaming the fall of mankind due to Original Sin on a woman for the last 3,000 years, so I suppose this phenomenon is no different.

8

The Mother Wound

"Mother is the word for God on the lips
and hearts of all children."
- The Crow (1994)

THE MOTHER WOUND was a phrase coined to describe the results of what occurs when a child does not experience a warm, caring connection with their mother. There are many different causes of this lack of connection. The mother could be chronically ill, be depressed, be bipolar, have schizophrenia, have PTSD, have a personality disorder, or be abusive, or they could be self- medicating with substances. Or, it could have nothing to do with illness; it could be the result of a single mother having to work two or more jobs and having no energy left at the end of the day to emotionally connect with her child/children. It could be none of these reasons and could simply be because she herself did not have a nurturing mother. Whatever the cause, the results are somewhat standard. The child will have anxiety around intimate relationships, have an inability to commit, could potentially develop borderline personality disorder, and have the inability to be loving and nurturing toward themselves or others.

Western society has also done a thorough job of criticizing a woman for being "only a homemaker," as if running a household wasn't hard work. And with the nature of today's economy, which makes it almost if not absolutely necessary for both parents to work, it is no wonder that our culture is collectively suffering from this often-unconscious Mother Wound.

Although I was not aware of the term Mother Wound until relatively recently, I became painfully aware of this dynamic at a very young age. In the arenas of psychology and self-help, it is said that if emotions are not dealt with consciously, they will reveal themselves eventually, often in destructive and harmful ways. My relationship with my Mother blatantly reflected this truth. Since from my conception, I was my Mother's "scarlet letter," she bore a certain level of resentment toward me and it became increasingly obvious the older I got. I remember as a young child that my Mom seemed to be much more nurturing and caring toward other children. I internalized this as a message that I was lesser than the other children and that she loved them more. I of course know now her behavior was a reflection of how she felt about herself and her life choices, maybe not even on a conscious level, and that she was projecting these feelings onto me. As I began to develop into a young woman, the contempt grew immensely. In fact, she had been "in love" with Neil , one of the man that kept me as his captive. At one point, after I escaped from the situation, she expressed how I had taken him for granted and that she would have loved him if she had been the one he was infatuated with, rather than expressing anger that a man was violating and abusing her teenage daughter.

As I explained earlier, my Mother and I were more like sisters than mother and daughter. However, rather than a rivalry it was more of... well, I can't really explain it. I would try harder to be better at everything, not to make her jealous, but rather in the hopes that she would show me love and acceptance. But the harder I tried, the more jealous she became. I recognize now that my Mother's emotional maturity had been stunted because of the abuse that she experienced as a child, and also that she was reacting to her own fear of not being loved, either by a man or by herself.

After my Grandmother passed away, a cousin in Missouri sent me some materials she had gathered during her genealogy research. Among the documents, I discovered several facts that appeared to be intentionally covered up. One of these facts was that after my Great-Grandfather on my maternal side had passed after serving in WWI, my Great- Grandmother would relinquish my Grandmother to the care of a St. Lois Catholic Boarding School every summer for several years so that she could go work in factories to support them. I often wonder, knowing what we now know about the abuse covered up by the Catholic Church, so who knows what went on in that boarding school that my Grandmother may have witnessed or experienced every summer. It appears that the Mother Wound may have been present in my family for several generations. Another interesting fact is that every woman on the maternal side of my family going back as far as I know to my Great-Great Grandmother, either had or died from heart issues. Of course genetics play a role, but in Eastern medicine, any physical heart conditions are considered to be caused by emotional heart conditions, which are usually related to grief, heartbreak, and the inability to forgive others. In the spring of 2014 I picked up a book at the library entitled "The Mother Wound." After skimming through it, it became obvious that I knew the phenomenon all too well. In late March I had a backpacking/hiking/camping adventure planned. I had met a friend of mine who was attending the local university and we headed out for the Gila National Forest. Friday afternoon, as we drove along the highway, we spotted an animal that had been hit along the side of the road and we both agreed that it would be best to go back to see if we could save it. Upon closer examination we realized it was a juvenile great horned owl, but it was too late, as its life had already expired. We gave the owl a ceremonial burial along that highway and left with a couple of feathers that she had gifted to us. I remember saying to my friend, "This is a significant sign…either you or I are about to experience a major life event." It's commonly believed that the owl represents wisdom and, in my experience, wisdom is most often found in the pain associated with death.

We went on with our weekend adventure as planned, but that was just the beginning of our encounters with Animal Medicine. Throughout the weekend, we encountered Raven, Gila Monster, and a large group of Doe and their Fawn. These weren't just your average sightings. As we sat taking a break from hiking enjoying a refreshing snack and some water, a crow swooped down and perched a couple of feet in front of me. He spread his wings and began to do the Crow Dance, undoubtedly asking for my attention. Throughout many Indigenous cultures, Raven/Crow medicine has been used by medicine people throughout the ages as a means to "shape shift." The art of shape shifting includes taking on another physical form, being in two places at one time, or becoming a "fly on the wall." I have also heard that the crow is the animal that escorts the soul in its transition at the time of death or serve as a Messenger for those that have already crossed over. Either explanation would be quite fitting. Next we were visited by a raven, who again swooped down and perched in front of me, performing no dance however, just perching and observing me quietly for what seemed like quite some time. The beautiful blue- black feathers of the raven represent the magic in the void. Raven medicine is said to give one the courage to enter that void, the darkness where The Great Mystery resides. When Raven visits you, it is said that you are about to experience a change in consciousness, but again these are things I that have been shared with me and every tribe has their own teachings.

The next day we ended up getting lost in the wilderness, not to the point where search and rescue needed to be called, but we certainly weren't where we had intended on being. As we were hiking back, retracing our steps, I caught something out of the corner of my eye and walked over to see what it might be. Perched out on a rock, enjoying the warmth of the sun, was a Gila monster. This probably wasn't too out of the ordinary, considering that we were in the Gila Wilderness, but when I crouched down he walked closer to me, which I perceived as being slightly peculiar. He even stayed long enough for a photo but decided that I had gotten a little too close for comfort when I attempted to touch him. And then he was gone. There is a tale about a snake and a lizard in some native cultures. Essentially, at the end of their conversation, the lizard tells the snake that he is not sleeping in the shade, but dreaming and that there is a distinct difference between the two. Lizard medicine tells one that they should be reverent of their dreams and recognize the wisdom that is being revealed in them, which as you may recall was something that my Grandmother had encouraged me to do as a young girl.

We finally made it out of the forest and back to the car. On our way out of the Gila Wilderness we saw a large herd of doe and their fawn on the grazing on the side of the road. We stopped the car and walked across the road slowly as not to startle them. Rather than bolting, they stayed put, watching us curiously. I continued to approach them so that I could get a better photo. As I drew closer, a doe that I had not seen stepped out from behind a large boulder. She took a couple of steps closer to me, her eyes locked with mine. She began to twitch her ears alternately, as if tapping a message in Morse code. Not once did they run from us, but rather stayed with us, as if they knew they were in no danger. It was we who decided to end the moment as it was getting late in the day and we still had a long drive ahead of us. Of all the animal medicine, I believe that this may be the most important of them all. Various Indigenous Tribes have a connection to the Deer Relatives. Many of the stories have to do with teachings of Gentleness, Love, Compassion, and even elements of Forgiveness which are not only qualities valued in most Indigenous cultures as well as Universal spiritual attributes. Often it is these very attributes that create a direct path or connection to Creator.

As we drove out of the canyon, the horizon revealed the most beautiful sunset I had ever seen. There were so many shades of pinks, purple, blues, reds, oranges, and yellows. And the clouds, the clouds were perfect. It literally looked as if someone had taken a paintbrush and lined the clouds with silver and gold. My friend Addison, an anthropologist who has studied the shamanic cultures of Central and

South America, turned to me and said that he had never seen anything like what he had just witnessed that weekend, that he was convinced that each one of those animals were trying to communicate something to me. It came as no surprise to me, as animal medicine has been a part of my path for quite some time. As we continued discussing what a remarkable weekend it was, my phone rang. It was my Uncle Mark. He called to tell me that my Mother had passed away that Friday night.

A year or so before that, I had decided that it was time that I forgave my Mother as well as make amends for the ways that I had hurt her. I had sent her a letter for her birthday with some small gifts and one extremely large gift. In the letter I told her that I had forgiven her and loved her no matter what, and that my offer still stood to help her get into a treatment center if she so chose.

Despite all the work that I had done in therapy around my Mother and our relationship, the moment the news of her death sank in, it was as if that work never happened. It felt as though the bandage had been ripped off and tequila and salt had been poured into my Mother Wound. All of the anger that I thought I had laid to rest came bubbling to the surface. "How dare she!" I exclaimed. "She didn't even fucking apologize or validate any of the ways that she had harmed me!" I think Addison was taken aback by my response to her death. The warm loving person that he had always known me to be instantly became the cold, callused person that I once was. Aside from that, Addison had lost his mother at a young age from a terminal illness, so undoubtedly witnessing my receiving this news must have triggered some deep feelings in him, whether he was conscious of them or not.

It was very late when I arrived home that night, but I couldn't sleep. I decided that I would feel better outside, under the stars. That is where I have felt the most at home my entire life. My cat and dog both followed me on this walk, but I didn't get very far. I sat on the railing of the pasture next to my house and I began to weep. Moments later, I was surrounded by three yearling colts, which really wasn't out of the ordinary, since I lived on the corner of a horse ranch, but the comfort that they showed me was extraordinary. Typically stud colts can be pretty aggressive, space-wise, and nippy at times, but not this time. One had his head rested on my shoulder, the other nuzzled my hair with his lip, and the third one nuzzled my thigh. I sat there weeping on a chilly spring night, under the stars, my cat and dog seated in front of me at my feet and the three horses behind me, lovingly showing their support in their silent, caring ways.

When I couldn't cry anymore, I decided to walk back home. When I got to my front door, there was an owl in the elm next to the house, "whoo-ing" at me, or at least that's what it felt like. I had heard that owls frequented the area, which of course made sense because I lived out in the farmlands, but that was the first time in the three, nearly four months that I had lived there, that I had seen or heard an owl. Another factor that made this experience so meaningful was that my Mother knew above all else how much I loved horses and had worked extremely hard to make my dream of owning a horse come true when I was a child. My Mom smoked crack for nearly two decades and had already suffered a heart attack as a side effect among many other devastating side effects, but she waited until I was living on a horse ranch, assisting with the foaling season, to transition on. I honestly couldn't think of a more loving and supportive place that I could have been.

I began making plans to travel to Florida. Whenever I travel, I try to avoid flying at all costs, not because I have a fear of flying or being hijacked by terrorists, but rather because I have a problem with constitutional rights being violated. So, I made plans to drive to Florida. I knew that dealing with the remaining members of my family, the house, the funeral, and all the awful memories that I would be flooded with would not be the most enjoyable thing in the world, so I intended on making the rest of the trip as enjoyable and meaningful as possible. On my way there I stopped at some of my Mom and my favorite places to visit. I stopped for barbecued ribs (my Mom's favorite) in Houston, I took photos in the Garden District of New Orleans, I stopped at Dauphin Island in Alabama and took a nap on the ancient Indian mounds, stopped at Pensacola beach, and eventually landed in Central Florida.

Just as I had imagined, the family home where she'd been living was dilapidated and beyond depressing. The filth and squalor that she lived in was sickening. I could barely stand to be in the house, but it had to be cleaned out so we could finally sell the dwelling that contained so many horrific memories. As I discarded the years worth of items that she hoarded, my resentment grew. After all the years of hard work of my Grandparents and the generations before them, this is what I had inherited – a kingdom of filth and generations of trauma! I was shocked when I found buried deeply in a china cabinet my Great-Grandmother's set of silverware, as anything of value had been stripped from that home and sold to get high a long, long time ago. We worked our way through the house. I eventually got to the office in the back of the house and there in the office, set aside in a pile, were my favorite paintings that my Grandmother had done, two archived copies of *National Geographic*, one from 1982 that featured the "Story Teller" Pueblo pottery on the cover (the year I was born along with my major in college) and the second featured yogic culture on the cover. Also found was the calligraphy set my Grandmother had given me when I was a child. These sentimental things had been set aside in an otherwise chaotic environment as if someone had been expecting me to come retrieve them. As I worked my way through the clutter of the office, I got to the last of the drawers of what had once been my Grandmother's dresser. In that bottom drawer I found a blue jewelry case. When I opened the case, inside I found a number of special items: my Great-Grandmother's string of pearls, a pair of my Grandmother's pearl earrings, my Mother's gold crucifix, a picture of me at nine years old, and $32.

At face value, these things may seem pretty random, but I immediately saw the meaning of it all. Two major events happened when I was nine years old: this was when my Mother became extremely ill. She had gone to the Catholic church that my family attended since she was a child to seek guidance from one of the priests. I'm not sure what actually happened there that day, but she came back in tears stating that she would never go back there again, and never did. I never saw her wear that crucifix again. Although I don't know the details, I am nearly positive that that was the day that she lost any remaining faith in her connection to Creator. This was also the year I was in fourth grade at the Catholic school I attended at the same church, which meant it was our turn to present the play reenacting the Stations of the Cross. As a devout Catholic, I wanted nothing more than to be given the role of the Virgin Mary, because she was so revered and virtuous, but I was also willing to take the role of Veronica. I prayed and prayed to Creator, negotiating the fact that I had suffered so much at such a young age that I had faith that He would reward me by giving me that honor. I got the role of Mary alright...Mary Magdalene. At that time, I didn't understand what that truly meant and what an honor that really was. All I knew was that I was targeted by the other children and laughed at because I was chosen to play the role of the prostitute, which was eerily foreshadowing. My Mother had taken a photo of me in costume after the Easter production and my Grandmother had done a painting of it. That was actually one of the paintings that had been set aside for me. Viewing it I was reminded of the sorrow I felt that day and how heavy my heart was at such a young age. That was the day that I decided that God hated me.

When I was a child, for my birthday I would receive the increment of money that was equivalent to the age I was turning. When I discovered this box which also contained $32, I was less than two months away from my 32nd birthday. As I sat there looking at the contents of this case experiencing a mixture of gratitude and disbelief, I suddenly remembered the day that my Grandmother had hidden it. It was around the time that she had had her leg amputated. I was in the office with her going on about how horrible her daughter was because she had just stolen a and pawned my Great-Grandmother's beautiful half-karat antique diamond ring that was set in platinum – something that my Grandmother had always said that I would inherit one day. As she hid those items in the box, she said to me, "I promise you that your Mother will not find these.

They are specifically for you and they will be waiting here for you when the day comes." She was right.

A couple of days after my Mother's funeral, I went back to the cemetery where she, my Grandmother, and my Great-Grandmother were all buried. I sat in prayer for quite some time and before I left I made a promise to them and to Creator that the trauma, poverty, and misfortune would end with me, that with Creator's help the family curse would once and for all be broken. While I was in Florida I connected with some of my dearest friends and got to make some much needed amends to people that I had hurt in my path of self-destruction.

With my car packed full of paintings, family keepsakes, and photos, my current K9 companion, Luna and I hit the road, headed back west. I stopped to spend a week with a couple of my beloved friends in southern Mississippi, where I received so much love, support, and southern hospitality. I stayed for Easter and had planned to leave the next day. After we enjoyed a huge Easter feast and were vegetating in their living room watching "Cosmos," I got the sudden inclination to check my email on my phone. With everything going on it was something I had neglected to do in the past couple of weeks. I saw that I had received an email from one of my uncles. Attached to the email was the scanned image of a hand-written letter from my Mother. It was dated January 1, 2014. In the letter she stated that she had been meaning to respond to my letter for the last year, how my words had inspired her to finally seek the healing that she needed. She went on to apologize for "the multitude of trials and tribulations" in our relationship. She wrote of how much she admired the woman I had become, strong and wise beyond my years, having attained a level of spirituality and maturity that most don't reach until their twilight years, if they are lucky enough to reach it. She went on to say that she felt big changes coming for our family, that this year would be the year that we would prosper. The letter trailed off into incoherent ramblings and nearly illegible handwriting. At the end of the letter was a phone number scribbled down for someone named "T-Lo," who I assume to be one of her many drug dealers, I assume. Needless to say, the letter was never finished, nor did she ever send it, but I got it nevertheless, which was a miracle in itself. How significantly symbolic! Her intentions Creator derailed by her all-consuming addiction, yet God filled in the gap, and on Easter, no less. The day which celebrates Christs resurrection was the day the mother-daughter love arose from the grave. Never had that quasi-Pagan/Christian Holiday ever held so much meaning for me.

I decided before leaving Mississippi that there was one more major mission that I needed to complete. I had to go to the French Quarter in New Orleans, to the site where Cain had first punched me in the face – to reclaim my power as a woman, the power that I gave away in that moment. So, I headed back to New Orleans. After finding the location of the incident, I stood there in prayer asking for Creator to always remind me of the immense strength and many gifts that He had given to me, so that I would never again feel the need to give away my power in an effort to be loved. Although there was a part of me that had always loved to nurture others, such as by cooking delicious meals for the ones I loved, I had lost that part of myself some time ago when I was still being abused and exploited by Cain. I left that spot as a renewed woman.

As I walked through the French Quarter, dodging droves of tourists from all of the states and the world, my eyes and heart began to see the downtrodden, sick, homeless inhabitants of the city, the ones that seemed invisible to everyone else. I have always had an affinity for help-ing the homeless, since I could identify with their affliction, by giving them money, buying them a hot meal, or taking a homeless mother to buy groceries for her children, but this was different. I turned my Nikon away from the architecture and street performers, and began asking those invisible lost souls if I could take their photos. They still asked for money, which due to travel and funeral expenses I had none, but I found that I was able to give them something far more valuable. I sat and listened to them, heard their stories, laughed with them, cried with them, prayed with them. I saw them for their souls and nothing more. Many thanked me, saying that they couldn't remember the last time that somebody showed them that they cared. The healing power of a nurturing woman had been awakened in me that day. Although the photos came out phenomenally and would most likely do very well at a gallery showing, I decided that some things are far more valuable than notoriety and money. Those photos represent human connection and unconditional love and will forever be a reminder to me of that day.

Before leaving New Orleans, I stopped at my favorite Creole restaurant, Coop's on Decatur Street. It's basically a little dirty dive bar, but they have the best sausage and rabbit gumbo, so Luna and I stopped for a bite to eat. As I sat there writing in my journal, enjoying a virgin mojito, I noticed a young woman sitting at the table across from me. We kept making eye contact and eventually she said something about what a beautiful dog I had (she is very striking in appearance, a huskie/timberwolf hybrid with perfect huskie markings and ice blue eyes). She eventually asked what I was writing, and I told her I was journaling, that I was making notes while writing my personal memoirs. She asked what they were about and I told her that I was a survivor of child sex trafficking and I had founded a non-profit to assist survivors in overcoming their trauma. She immediately got up from her table with tears in her eyes and came over and wrapped her arms around me. When she let go she looked at me and said that her boyfriend, a police officer in Chicago, had invited her to go on a ride-along, which resulted in her own experience of being trafficked, and that's how her daughter had been conceived. She thanked me for what I was doing and left the restaurant. Luna and I sat there enjoying our food, as I rested in the fact that I had just gotten another one of those road signs from Creator that I was indeed on the right path.

Returning to my home on the ranch (where, by the way, many things are made of horseshoes), I realized that I was in fact coming home...not necessarily my permanent home, but rather the place where I was finally coming home to myself. Through Creator's perfectly planned series of synchronicities, I was able to find the magic in the darkness, the Great Mystery. And through these events I realized that that deep painful Mother Wound that I had carried with me all these years had finally been healed.

9

Another Girl Interrupted

"Feminist writers warned psychiatric drugs could silence women, as asylums had. Antidepressants have since overshadowed minor tranquilizers. Psychiatrists, many of them women, remain mindful of this history."
- The Science Museum Women and Psychiatry

WHEN I WAS twelve, I read the book *Girl Interrupted*, which would later become a popular movie starring Wynona Rider and Angelina Jolie. The book was the personal memoirs of Suzanne Kaysen, which recorded and recounted her experience of being institutionalized for a suicide attempt. After reading the book I didn't feel so alone, because by that age I had already experienced my first attempt at suicide. On the eve of my twelfth birthday, I took a bottle of pills and cut my wrists with a razor. Neither of these actions were severe enough to be fatal, but they were certainly a cry for help, and I lived my life for the next thirteen years in a chronically suicidal state, each attempt becoming more and more potentially lethal. Really, my whole life for that thirteen-year period was one big suicide attempt. I lived as though I wanted to die, because I did. Life had absolutely no value or meaning.

Since life is lived forward and understood backward, sometimes it takes me a while to connect the dots. I thought that this topic deserved an entire chapter rather than getting lost in the fabric of the story, since our country is currently experiencing a collective mental health crisis.

I was first taken to counseling when I was about nine years old. I am pretty sure it happened as a result of my teacher reporting concerns about my behavior and the sorry excuse for a child welfare investigation into my family. Since the "investigation" yielded no conclusive evidence, then it *obviously* had to be something wrong with me. These counseling sessions were uncomfortable, awkward, and pointless. They were at a family center. The counselor was an older balding man with bifocal tinted glasses, who seemed like he was stuck back sometime in the seventies. The room was sterile and uninviting. I remember hating having to go, since deep down inside I knew that I was not the problem. However, it felt like I was the one being punished by being scrutinized in these sessions, which by the way didn't integrate any of the tools that are effective when counseling children. I'm not sure if it was because techniques such as sand tray therapy, art therapy, and psychodrama had not yet been integrated into mainstream counseling, or if the counselor I was seeing just didn't know what he was doing. Unfortunately that happens in every industry.

Shortly after starting counseling it was recommended that I be put on Paxil to relieve my symptoms of "social anxiety." It wasn't long after beginning this psychotropic medication that I started having suicidal thoughts, and not long after that I began acting on those impulses. In fact, I started having all types of impulsive behavior and less control over my emotional states and reactions. After my first suicide attempt, my dosage of Paxil was increased, "because it was obvious the medication wasn't working." My second suicide attempt a few months later involved my consuming an entire bottle of my Paxil prescription. I had a heart murmur for years after that as a result. After Paxil, then it was Zoloft, and after Zoloft it was Prozac, and after Prozac it was Serzone, and on and on...and my suicidal behavior and depression continued. It was no wonder I believed that reaching for something outside of myself could change the way I felt. After I was conditioned to be a drug seeker, I began using street drugs.

Some people may still argue that there is a difference; that prescription drugs are doctor- prescribed and so are therefore safer and the consumption is justified. There is a huge difference in the safety quotient. Street drugs are by far safer than prescription drugs have proven to be. Depressants, opioids and antidepressants are responsible for more overdose deaths (45%) than cocaine, heroin, methamphetamine and amphetamines (39%) combined.[10]

I am by no means advocating for the use of street drugs, but I have to say when the "black label" law (suicide warning on antidepressants when prescribed to teenagers) became a FDA requirement in 2005, I can't say I was surprised. When I was seventeen, I made the choice that I wasn't going to take anymore doctor-prescribed psychotropic drugs. They just didn't work for me.

At nineteen years old I began experiencing troublesome trauma symptoms, such as nightmares, inability to sleep, mood swings, and a slew of other symptoms that I didn't have the vocabulary for at the time. I went to see a psychiatric nurse practitioner and she thought that I was experiencing symptoms of bipolar disorder. After much persuasion from the nurse practitioner, I went against my best judgement and left with a prescription for a medication named Zyprexa, which I was told was an antidepressant that would help with my nightmares and other symptoms. The first couple of days on the medication I was completely sedated, sleeping upwards of nineteen hours a day. I worked at Hard Rock Café at the time and even my supervisors thought that I was under the influence of something. I called the medical professional to report the side effects. She responded that it would take a little time for my body to adjust to the medication, just to stick with it and I should feel better within three weeks. A couple days later

---

10   Foundation for a Drug Free World http://www.drugfreeworld.org/drugfacts/prescription/abuse-international-statistics.html

I ended up with a head trauma as a result of losing consciousness from the medication. After I drove home from work one night, I got out of my truck, suddenly feeling very dizzy. I took one step forward to walk toward my apartment door and passed out, falling face-first on the concrete. I don't know how long I had lost consciousness. When I came to face down on the concrete in the parking lot, it must've been sometime in the middle of the night. I could feel a gaping wound above my left eye, but all the blood had dried. Still dizzy and discombobulated, I let myself into my apartment, made my way upstairs and crawled into bed. The next day I was too afraid to go to a doctor to get stitches as I no longer felt that medical professionals had my best interest in mind after that experience with the nurse practitioner, so I put butterfly bandages on my wounds and immediately ceased taking the medication. Afterward, I did my own research, only to find out that this specific medication was *actually* an antipsychotic, and one of the side effects was the risk of lowering the blood pressure so severely that it could cause one to lose consciousness.

After this experience I had a profound distrust for the medical and pharmaceutical industries. I stayed away from doctors for a few years until I signed up for a Preferred Provider Organization (PPO) insurance policy. For some reason I felt safer if I could choose the doctor that I wanted. Even if they were out of network, I would have a better experience this time around. The primary care physician I chose, who came highly recommended to me, was wonderful. He was intelligent, respectful, had great bedside manner, and was quite handsome. After seeing him for several months for random but chronic pain, digestion issues, sleeping problems, anxiety, and muscle tension, I left with quite the cocktail of prescription medications: Lexapro, Xanax, Nexium, Trazadone, Flexril and Soma. Not long after starting the cocktail, I had a petit mal seizure while driving. It was a very frightening experience. After going back to consult with my doctor about the side effect, he made the decision to switch me over to another Selective Serotonin Reuptake Inhibitor (SSRI) called Effexor. After being on Effexor for a few weeks, I became so depressed that I was too depressed to even think about suicide, because it would take far too much effort. It was hard enough to peel myself off of the couch to go to work. At that point I was taking 75 mg of the drug. When I went back in for a follow-up and told the doctor about the current side effects that I was experiencing, he explained to me that I was experiencing serotonin syndrome and that this could be resolved by adjusting my dosage. I left that day with a prescription of Effexor for 150 mg. Shortly after I started that dosage, I began experiencing tardive dyskinesia, an involuntary muscular movement in my limbs. A coworker noticed my arm jerking around one day on a cigarette break. He asked me what was going on. I explained the situation briefly to him. His reaction cued me in on exactly how insane this whole situation was. My next appointment with that doctor, I asked if I could stop taking it, to which he replied something to the effect of, "Yes and no. Yes we can begin to wean you off of the drug, but to stop taking it cold turkey would be too dangerous as it would likely cause seizures." I think it was at that point that I finally began to realize that it was a systemic crisis developing in healthcare, that doctors were putting aside their Hippocratic Oath to become glorified drug pushers, whether or not it was in the patient's best interest.

For quite a while I thought that I was just extremely sensitive to these types of drugs, but as I read more and more articles and talked to more and more people about their experiences, I began to realize that these drugs are inherently dangerous. These stories aren't highly publicized, and neither is the research that has been done that indicates the inherent dangers of psychotropic medications.[11] However, upon further research you will find no shortage of stories of individuals who were prescribed hypnotic drugs like Ambien or Remeron, who under the influence of the drugs, committed crimes that they have no recollection of, such as vehicular manslaughter or opening fire in a retirement home and killing several individuals.[12] One study concluded that shooters in the majority of school shootings were on some type of

11   12 Shocking Facts About the Dangers of Psychiatric Drugs http://www.globalhealingcenter.com/natural-health/12-shocking-facts-psychiatric-drugs/

12   The Disturbing Side Effect of Ambien http://www.huffingtonpost.com/2014/01/15/ambien-side-effect-sleepwalking-sleep-aid_n_4589743.html

psychotropic drug or combination of drugs.[13] The most disturbing recent story in the news allegedly involving psychotropic drugs, was the
tragic suicide of Robin Williams. According to the CCHR International
Mental Health Watch Dog, two weeks prior to his death, Robin Williams
was prescribed Seroquel and Remeron, this information was released
from the toxicology report of his autopsy. Of course, it seemed that
that detail of his death was not highly publicized.

According to the Harvard Center for Ethics: "Few know that sys-
tematic reviews of hospital charts found that even properly prescribed
drugs (aside from mis-prescribing, overdosing, or self-prescribing)
cause about 1.9 million hospitalizations a year. Another 840,000 hos-
pitalized patients are given drugs that cause serious adverse reactions for a total of 2.74 million serious adverse drug reactions. About
128,000 people die from drugs prescribed to them. This makes prescription drugs a major health risk, ranking 4th with stroke as a leading cause of death. The European Commission estimates that adverse
reactions from prescription drugs cause 200,000 deaths; so together,
about 328,000 patients in the U.S. and Europe die from prescription
drugs each year. The FDA does not acknowledge these facts and instead gathers a small fraction of the cases."

Again, the US population only makes a small percentage of the
world population, however we are responsible for consuming the majority of pharmaceutical drugs worldwide. Is this because we have the
most superior healthcare system in the world? No – in fact, our healthcare system is far from superior when compared to those in other
developed nations. What we do have, however, is an out-of-control,
rogue pharmaceutical industry that has incredibly too much influence and power over our government. And if one were to study the
history of biomedical ethics in the United States, one would quickly
realize that through the advent of managed care in our healthcare system, doctors were put into a position where it would be nearly, if not

---

13   Gun News-Rifle Manufacturer John Noveske Mysteriously Killed After Posting Con-
     troversial Article
     http://www.texasgopvote.com/issues/stop-big-government/gun-news-rifle-manu-
     facturer-John-Noveske-mysteriously-killed-shortly-after-005014

absolutely necessary for them to accept bonuses from pharmaceutical companies for peddling their goods. It turns out that there is quite an incentive for pushing these dangerous drugs. If you want to know the truth, follow the money trail. The healthcare industry is no exception to this rule.

Recently I went to see my doctor to discuss how I was recovering from my most recent PTSD episode. After explaining that I was struggling with some symptoms since I have not been able to keep a supply of medical cannabis on hand (due to my low finances and the increase in taxes on the medication), the doctor asked me if I had tried benzodiazepines before, to which I replied, "yes, I was prescribed and addicted to them for years." We had a long conversation in which I basically stated that I had read in several European medical journals that they were an effective treatment option when used in extremely low dosages for a very short period of time, but that prolonged use not only posed the risk of addiction but also was inherently damaging to the nervous system. I explicitly stated that I would be comfortable trying the lowest dosage available (0.25 mg) and only a two-week supply, so no more than a quantity of fourteen. When I received my paperwork and prescriptions from the front desk, she had written a prescription of Xanax, a thirty-day supply (quantity of thirty) with a dosage of 0.5 mg daily, with two refills. The amount that I requested of this highly addictive substance was a cumulative of 3.5 mg over a two-week period, but instead the doctor insisted on giving me a cumulative amount of 45 mg. Why would medical professionals do such a thing unless there wasn't some type of incentive? What happened to the main tenet of the Hippocratic Oath to do no harm?

Another thing I feel is imperative to look at when discussing "mental illness" is the way in which it is being dealt with in the United States. Despite the mass consumption of prescription drugs in this country, many of which are of a psychotropic nature, there is a huge stigma that exists around mental illness. Even though high percentages of our population have at least one psychiatric diagnosis, it is the social leprosy of our culture. There is a still a taboo around speaking about it.

When mental illness is a detail in a mass shooting, the news networks tend to sensationalize, even demonize that detail, without mentioning the cocktail of medications the individual was prescribed whose side effects include impulsive behaviors, homicidal/suicidal thoughts and/ or behavior, psychosis, etc. Within this context we have two essential elements at play: our old friend shame and a red herring. I would even go as far as to say there are more deaths associated with medications being the cause, rather than mental illness itself.

Many of the people suffering with the most severe cases of mental illness end up in one of three places: on the streets, in correctional facilities, or dead. I have read countless disturbing stories over the past year of law enforcement using excessive and often deadly force on individuals with mental illness, not because they had to, but because this type of behavior is being permitted by law enforcement agencies across the country. In cities across the nation, homeless people are brutalized and murdered by encounters with violent youth. There is even the trend of new legislation emerging that deems it unlawful to feed the homeless. People in need of the most care are being consistently degraded and treated in a subhuman fashion. This could easily be me. What it I hadn't had the self-awareness to realize that the medication doctors were pushing on me were actually making my symptoms worse? What if I continued taking those drugs and ended up wandering the streets talking to myself? I could just as easily become the next nameless, faceless fatality in this society that seems to have lost all sense of compassion.

I could write volumes on ways upon which our current behavioral health system could be improved, but that is for another time. I learned more in five minutes from my first Kundalini Yoga teacher, Gurumeet Kaur, than I learned in twenty years from countless mental health professionals about the imbalances that I had experienced throughout my life. Without my telling her many, if any, details of my life, she described my childhood self perfectly. She identified the biggest challenges I had faced in my life such as the fact that I was highly intelligent, but struggled in conventional school settings, have always had issues with authority such as being told what to believe, have always been extremely big-hearted and had heightened emotional sensitivity, and that I have always struggled with feeling like I never belonged and as a result struggled with suicidality. I was shocked that she knew so much about me, as I had only taken her class for a semester. I asked her how she knew all of those things and she told me that I was an Indigo child, adding that when these types of children do not have the proper environment that supports their creativity and emotional needs, they become *extremely* self-destructive, typically turning to drugs or alcohol as a method to destroy themselves. This state of being an Indigo child simply referred to an imbalance in the chakra system, that this was in fact the cause for nearly all illness and disease and could therefore be put into balance and restored to a place of homeostasis. And she was right.

Although replacing medications with a daily discipline of Kundalini Yoga and meditation takes far more commitment and work than popping a pill out of a bottle, I have experienced exponentially more powerful results in healing and symptom management. I have a sense of exactly what my mind and body need when they are out of balance. I realized through my experience of transitioning from allopathic medicine to a holistic lifestyle, the key to healing is to begin with the Soul. Once you begin working with the Soul, the mind and body follow suite in the healing process. Do I still experience symptoms of PTSD? Yes. Are there still days that I completely fall apart? Sometimes. But these interruptions are fewer and farther between, and when these symptoms raise their ugly head, this woman gives a lot less of her time to the interruption.

10

Play It Again, Sam

*"There are only patterns, patterns on top of patterns,
patterns that affect other patterns. Patterns hidden by
patterns. Patterns within patterns. If you watch close,
history does nothing but repeat itself. What we call chaos
is just patterns we haven't recognized. What we call
random is just patterns we can't decipher. What we can't
understand we call nonsense. What we can't read we call
gibberish. There is no free will. There are no variables."*

- Chuck Palahniuk, Survivor

HISTORY HAS A tendency to repeat itself, especially when the inherent wisdom it contains is ignored. Life is by far anything but linear and static. There is a Sanskrit word, *samskara,* which translates to impressions and being under the influence of previous impressions, of experiences generated in this life or possibly even previous ones, if reincarnation is a part of your perspective. Interestingly enough, neuroscience and the emerging field of behavioral epigenetics is just beginning to catch up with this 10,000-year-old insight.

Neuroscience contends that negative experiences make deeper grooves, if you will, on the human brain. Think of the brain like a record player – that near-obsolete technology that once played vinyl records. Since the grooves that are created by negative experiences are by nature deeper than the grooves created by positive or even neutral experiences, the needle of the phonograph tends to get stuck in the grooves created by these negative experiences; therefore, one tends to stay under the influence of the specific impression. I can completely attest to the tendency to subconsciously recreate and attract individuals into my life that are capable of recreating the trauma that I experienced earlier in my life. Because this tendency was completely subconscious, I was under the impression that I was cursed, had the worst "luck" imaginable, and was powerless. Simply a victim of circumstances, I believed that the Creator simply hated me.

Once I made the declaration that I was going to do whatever it took to heal and began praying doors would open in my life, my life began to change. All these pathways to healing began to emerge in my life. As I continued to increase my commitment to my healing, I became more and more conscious of the ways in which I was perpetuating my own suffering, essentially victimizing myself or allowing others to victimize me. When I began working professionally with other survivors of sex trafficking, I noticed the same quality in their choices and behavior. When others expressed their frustration and lack of understanding in this cycle of ongoing self-destruction and "poor decision making," I sat in silence, simply identifying with that helpless feeling of being under the influence of that seemingly inescapable cycle.

As my Kundalini Yoga and meditation practice grew, so did I, so did my understanding, and so did my consciousness. I became more aware of the decisions that I was making in my life that only perpetuated my suffering and moment by moment, I began to make decisions from a place of greater clarity, greater self-worth...from a place of responding with love rather than reacting out of habituation. As this process continued to unfold in my own life, I was able to assist others in finding a way out of their own self-destructive habituation. The experience of watching another human being step out of the cycles in their lives which held them hostage is by far the most beautiful thing that I have ever witnessed, much like the blooming of a rare, beautiful, fragrant flower.

But what of ancestral trauma? It wasn't until 1980 that PTSD became officially recognized as a diagnosis, so research into historical trauma and it's lasting effecting on individuals, families, and communities is still relatively new. However, the emerging field of behavioral epigenetics is beginning to shine light onto how trauma in previous generations continues to affect the descendants and their biology. Before the emergence of the epigenetic theory, the psychology community was in a constant debate over nature versus nurture. Well, it turns out proponents of both sides of the argument were correct. Our environment and the experiences within that environment have the ability to alter our DNA through a biological chemical reaction of methylation. These methyl groups reside next to strands of DNA and act as book-markers if you will, marking what genes need to be activated for that cell's specific purpose. Since the brain of the human infant does 90 percent of its developing after birth in the first year of life, the environment of the infant and the disposition of the infant's caregivers are absolutely imperative to the development of said infant's brain. Gabor Mate, MD and his team of researchers have developed a theory based on this information: "if an infant does not have at least one attentive, emotionally connected, and reasonably non-stressed caregiver" in their life, their dopamine reward system found in the limbic area of the brain does not develop correctly. Dopamine is the neurotransmitter that regulates movement and emotional responses, and it enables us not only to see rewards, but to take action to move toward them. Low dopamine levels are consistently associated with addiction, as individuals constantly seek stimulus from the outside to increase these dopamine levels. The good news is that if these genes can be manipulated in a way that is damaging to the biology of the individual, they can also be manipulated in a way that is beneficial for the individual through many different approaches including diet, exercise, love and support, spiritual practices, sound therapy, etc.

"The genome has long been known to be the blueprint of life, but the epigenome is life's Etch A Sketch: Shake it hard enough and you can wipe clean any family curse."
- Discover Magazine, May 2013, "Grandma's Experiences Leave a Mark on Your Genes"

In my case it was Kundalini Yoga that shook me hard enough. For more than six years I had struggled to make lasting changes in my life through attempting to change my behavior, attempting to think positively, attempting to change my diet, attempting to meditate, and so on. But nothing stuck. For six years I continually fell into the same self-destructive cycles, no matter what I changed on the outside. When I began my Teacher Training course to become a certified Kundalini Yoga teacher, I was told that by adhering to the path of Kundalini Yoga, which embodied all eight limbs of Yoga, according to Pantajali, I would in fact not only heal my own DNA, but I would also heal my family lineage seven generations to the future and seven generations to the past. Upon hearing this, I was of course skeptical, until one day when I was having a conversation with one of my uncles and he said to me, "I used to think that this family was cursed and that I was cursed being born into this family, but because of who you have become and what you are doing in your life I feel extremely blessed and as though you have blessed our entire family." That was the only confirmation I needed. Kundalini Yoga connected my mind, body, and spirit with Creator and through Creator/Spirit all healing is possible.

So just as it was imperative for me to look at my family's history to understand the curse that had been passed on for generations, I believe that it is equally imperative to examine the history of slavery and all the societal implications that come with it if we are ever going to find a solution and cure for the epidemic of human trafficking.

Part 3

Status Quo: To Change or Accept More of the Same?

The Ugly Truth

"Those who do not learn from history
are doomed to repeat it."
– George Santayana

LET'S FACE IT...SLAVERY has existed nearly as long as mankind itself. Once one tribe or nation decided that for some reason they were superior to another and could dominate them by brute force, slavery came into existence. The way in which people are dominated, suppressed, and trafficked has changed over the ages, but the fact is there are more people trapped in slavery today than there ever have been throughout history.[14] Of course, this is a reflection of the exponential growth of the human population, but one would think that with the advent of human rights, technology, and the abolition of slavery in countries all over the world that we had somehow evolved out of this behavior. Sadly, we have not.

In the United States alone, human trafficking is a $32 billion a year industry in which an estimated 100,000 children are trafficked annually (although these figures are under scrutiny), and experts contend

---

14 BBC News Magazine, October 2012, "A Tipping Point in the Fight Against Slavery"

that this number is not a true representation of the actual numbers because this number only reflects the number of cases *reported*. Since the World Cup that was hosted in Germany in 2006, the media has given an increasing amount of focus to the connection between mega sporting events, human trafficking, and child sexual exploitation. This is not a phenomenon that just began occurring, either. My experience happened over twenty years ago. I also know another child sex trafficking survivor who is in her sixties. I have seen a black-and- white photo from the 1930s, during the era of the Great Depression, of a woman holding a sign offering her children for sale. And what of child sex trafficking in third-world countries? We have, as a developed nation, known of child sex tourism in places such as India, Thailand, the Philippines, etc. for decades. It was just one of those problems that we liked to think of that happened "to them, somewhere over there." But, now that we know it is happening here to our American children, and politicians have decided to begin using this topic as a political platform, we are obligated to examine this issue.

Just as I have found many jewels of self-knowledge in the darkest places of my own life, I believe that we as a culture have much to learn about ourselves by examining this issue. In a recent study, it has been discovered that child sex trafficking is a $343 billion industry in India. I believe that that figure deserves to be repeated. The sale of small children in India for the perverse sexual pleasure of others, mostly men, is an industry that brings in **$343 billion**. Why have Americans not intervened more in this issue? Why did it only begin to matter when we discovered it was happening to our children too? Do American children possess more of an intrinsic value than other children around the world? Are we not all created by the same Creator and of the same organic materials?

It is not just children. Women around the world are exploited daily...kidnapped, offered job opportunities that only turn out to be bait, exploited and manipulated through death threats, their children held hostage as leverage. The more truth you know, the uglier it gets. So, who is responsible for this ugliness?

It would be so much easier if we could just point a finger at the bad guy, but for an issue to become as pervasive as this one, everyone is a willing participant. Crimes such as this depend on the indifference of good people. Going from here I believe there are four essential questions that need to be examined: What is the worldview of women and children? What is the worldview on slavery? What societal characteristics perpetuate these crimes? Why does a market for this even exist?

Let us begin with the story of Original Sin. Adam and Eve are in Paradise. Eve wanders off on a walk and is tempted by the Devil, who has cleverly disguised himself as a talking snake. The talking snake convinces Eve to eat the forbidden fruit from the Tree of Knowledge of Good and Evil. Woman is responsible for the fall of mankind. I chose this example because Christianity is one of the largest religions in the world and being raised Catholic (now recovering), it is one of those myths that I am most familiar with. It is also my understanding that the advent of the three Abrahamic religions was the first occasion in history where there was no recognition of the Divine female aspect of Creator or Creation. Fast-forward several millennia to look at Latin anatomy and physiology. The Latin word for a woman's vulva is "pudendum" which translates to "that which is to be ashamed of." Recent sociological studies cite that females ranking in a higher socioeconomic class have adopted the practice of "slut-shaming" as a method of maintaining a social status quo in colleges and universities across the United States. It seems that shaming is a very powerful tool when used to suppress another group. Why wouldn't it be? It directly attacks an individual's sense of self-worth and when one feels they are not worth anything better, then why would they challenge the status quo?

In addition to the lens through which woman has been viewed through throughout history, there is the next obvious contribution to a world culture that is infected with the crime of human trafficking: the treatment of children. Only in the last century were child labor laws created, and that was here in a developed country. In some countries, children witness as their entire family is slaughtered and are then trained to use machine guns and kill others in war. Within this spectrum there are different levels of child abuse, neglect, and exploitation. If women are the second-class citizens of the world, then children are the third class. Even in a country as wealthy as the United States, the funding that is budgeted or the care and welfare of women and children is constantly under attack, leaving already vulnerable populations even more vulnerable.

As someone who has experienced first-hand and professionally studied the industry of human trafficking, the main thing that a trafficker seeks out is a vulnerable person. Vulnerable people make easy prey. They are starved of the essentials in life: love, care, finances, food, protection, etc. It doesn't require much effort on the predator's part to exploit a vulnerable person, as their trust can be won over very easily. This is not the victim's fault. It's a tragic declaration, but victim blaming is very prevalent. Love and trust are essential aspects of the whole person. When an infant or child is shown love, they naturally form a trusting relationship with that caregiver. If this were not supposed to occur, we would not have been created this way. When a vulnerable person trusts a predator, it is often because they were shown some form of affection or love. I personally struggled with working with clients that presented with symptoms of Stockholm syndrome, the condition in which a victim has sentiments of love for or dependence on their offender. After a few years of working with other trafficking survivors, what bothered me the most was that I, too, had had some of the same emotion toward my offenders, but I had been in denial for years. It was that feeling of receiving what I thought was love that led me to trusting those individuals, all starting from that experience of their pretending that they "cared" about me. This is what law enforcement and other experts have come to call "grooming", acting in such a way to make a person feel safe and cared for so that they are more easily coerced and manipulated.

If you believe that welfare benefits should be cut or shouldn't exist, you are essentially contributing to the trade of human trafficking, because this is an industry that preys on vulnerable populations and food sovereignty is connected with the crime of sex trafficking. We human beings are each unique in our own sense, but there are a few things that we all have in common and one of those needs is to eat. Being that our country was founded as a democratic republic, I believe that these programs should be run on the state level so they better reflect the needs of the residents in that state. Sadly, though, it seems that our government no longer serves the people and hasn't for quite some time.

Although it seems that my last statement may have been directed toward conservatives, I want to explicitly state that *everyone* is responsible for this horrific crime. In this country, on one end of the spectrum we have neo-conservativism, which only recognizes life in the womb as being sacred. All other life can fend for itself, be sentenced to death if sanctioned by the state, and be killed in warfare, so long as it is somehow justified. On the other end of the spectrum is neoliberalism, where absolutely *nothing* is sacred. Everything is marketable in the name of profit. Within this belief system, moving towards privatization is viewed as a good thing.

A perfect example of this is the privatized prison system in the United States. As some of you may recall, during the Reagan era, state-run sanitariums were shut down, resulting in an increase in the mentally ill homeless population. Corporations eventually got together and figured out a way to make a profit off of these vulnerable people. The privatized prison system became big business. The U.S. boasts the highest number of imprisoned people worldwide, even including our Communist neighbors. Among the imprisoned, 65 percent of the inmates meet medical criteria for severe mental health and substance abuse problems.[15] Really think about that for a moment...over half of inmates in U.S. prisons are being punished for being sick. Yes, often there is a crime that they have committed that that precipitated their arrest, but in most cases these crimes could have been prevented with the proper resources put in place within our society. But, because we live in a so-called "Christian nation" that refuses to love their neighbor, we do not make these resources available. Thus, as a result of us not

---

15   US Department of Justice's Bureau of Justice Statistics

adequately caring for and protecting vulnerable populations, corporations now exploit them for profit, through the privatized prison system and forced labor, which by definition is a form of human trafficking.

To illustrate what these principles look like, we can turn to the case of Sara Kruzan, who grew up in Riverside, California. She was a bright, young, promising girl, like me and many other victims of sex trafficking. Her mother was a single working parent, her father having been sentenced to a long prison term. At eleven years old, Sara met a trafficker who played the role of a surrogate father in her life. Two years later he began trafficking her for sex. By age sixteen, she grew tired of the rapes, the beatings, the humiliation, and the dehumanization that comes along with being trafficked. Sara shot and killed her offender. Only then did the state intervene with a decisive action. In 1994, at seventeen years old, Sara was adjudicated as an adult and sentenced to life in prison without parole. Despite full disclosure of the events surrounding this crime, the district attorney opted to ignore her pleas for extenuating circumstances and have her convicted to the full extent of the law. Keep in mind that this prison is paid for every day that she is incarcerated. Eventually, Sara Kruzan's case drew a lot of media attention, which resulted in a significant amount of public outcry. In 2001, California's governor, Arnold Schwarzenegger, amended her sentence, reducing it to twenty-five years with the opportunity to be released on parole. Not only was this vulnerable child exploited and abused by her offender, she was later exploited and abused by the judicial system and exposed to who knows what type of abuses while in prison. More recently the story of Cyntonia Brown of Tennessee surfaced on social media. The details of the stories are very similar. Both young women of color, both sixteen years old, both sentenced to life for shooting their offenders as they were being victimized in child sex trafficking. Cyntonia was recently released to probation by the state of Tennessee after social influencers took interest and bolstered the years of advocacy and public outcry but only after serving 14 years of her life sentence.

This is not the only time this type of scenario has occurred. Another survivor of child sex trafficking was sold into the pornography industry to star in a snuff film (the type of pornography in which the woman is murdered). After being nearly strangled to death with a noose, she took her first opportunity to shoot her offender when an altercation broke out on the set. The fact is, this type of injustice has occurred more times than we would like to admit and still continues in states that have not yet adopted the Safe Harbor Law, a legislation created in 2011 to protect minors from being prosecuted if they are victims of sex trafficking.

Another example of the corruption and exploitation of vulnerable people by our system: a judge in the juvenile courts of Massachusetts who was eventually was caught after a decade of accepting tens of thousands of dollars in kickbacks from a privatized juvenile detention facility for giving every teen that passed through his court the maximum sentence possible. Since the development of the Safe Harbor law that protects minors from being prosecuted for being trafficked was not created until 2011, this judge very likely had at least one if not multiple victims of child sex trafficking come through his court. After being sold and bought by street criminals, they experienced being sold by a person in a position of authority whose duty it was to protect their best interest. But because this public official was corrupted by money, these adolescents' lives were only further destroyed. We will never know just how much damage he caused in the lives of these individuals.

Of course, there are the more covert injustices, such as those in my case. Rather than take out my rage on my offenders, I internalized the anger and sought out the most destructive choices that I could possibly make, many of which were illegal and included abusing substances. As you may recall, I was sent to substance abuse treatment by the juvenile courts as a means of ensuring my well-being, but substance abuse was only a symptom of the greater problem. The root of the problem was the trauma that I had experienced not just being trafficked but dating all the way back to three years old when I first remembered the sexual abuse my family home. Throughout history it has been quite obvious that when something goes wrong in an individual's life, the approach has been, "what's wrong with you?" While walking my path of healing and walking alongside others on their paths of healing, I have discovered a far more effective approach found in asking, "what happened to you," followed by compassionate listening. Once you have heard an individual's story, while doing your best to withhold judgment, obviously the following question should be, "how can I help you heal?" This is only beginning to become our reality in the clinical sector alone, thanks to advances in trauma-informed care and the research that Lisa Najavits, Ph.D. of Harvard University has done in her research on the connection between trauma and substance abuse, as well as her research of how women recover differently from men in regard to trauma and substance abuse. This brings up a good point: Alcoholics Anonymous was founded in 1933. Since then, all research on alcoholism and drug addiction has focused on men, following the line of thought that the findings could equally be applied to women. However, this is not the case. Dr. Najavits was the first researcher to revolutionize the way we approach helping women to recover from trauma and substance dependence...*six decades* after the founding of AA...for someone to consider the specific needs of women to fully recover from trauma and substance abuse. How many women and men are sitting in prison right now or have previously served sentences, with substance abuse problems or mental health issues that are a result of unaddressed trauma? After all, the Adverse Childhood Experiences study links as little as a single episode of abuse or neglect as a child to risky behavior (as well as other negative outcomes), which can often result in incarceration. I dare to say the number is in the millions, and it is only by the grace of Creator that I am not part of that heartbreaking statistic.

Earlier, I mentioned how the child welfare system in Florida failed me for years by not removing me from the abusive environment that I grew up in. But what of the children that are rescued by child protective services? Do they stand a better chance? Are they at less risk of being trafficked? Sadly, the answer is no. This system is far beyond broken, as well. Many children are placed in abusive foster homes and in an attempt to escape, find themselves just as vulnerable to would-be traffickers. Even worse, child sex traffickers have figured out that the best way to gain access to vulnerable youth is by assuming un-suspected positions within the community including, but certainly not limited to, foster families.

In 2013, I accepted the position of Program Director at an agency that provided services for at-risk youth in Northern New Mexico. Not only was this agency out of compliance with all of the sources that provided them funding through their grants, but the agency also had made no effort to collaborate with other agencies in town that were promoting anti-trafficking initiatives. Because the youth we served were prime targets of trafficking predators, I made the evolution of the agency's culture one of my primary goals when I accepted the job. It turned out to be a much bigger hurdle than I thought it would be.

While I was working 55-60 hours a week to bring the program back up to some form of acceptable standards, I also pushed for educa-tion around the prevention of child sex trafficking. I advocated for the agency to begin accepting referrals for victims of child sex trafficking, as at that time they were turning those adolescents away, and there was not another agency in the state that was willing to work with them. I was shocked by the opposition I received around these efforts. I was blessed to have an incredible team that worked with me, but the level of dysfunction within the administrative staff was indescrib-able. The clinical supervisor of the agency was a nightmare. In clinical meetings she would make fun of clients in front of staff by mimicking their cries for help. She would condescend these vulnerable youths to their faces, telling them that they needed to reevaluate their goals simply because she didn't believe in their ability to accomplish them. She consistently overrode my decisions or criticized my decisions to accept clients because she considered them "throwaways" that would not make our program look good. Her behavior had reached such a destructive level that staff no longer wanted to attend clinical meet-ings, clients completely shut down, unwilling to participate as a result of this emotional and psychological abuse. This individual was my direct supervisor, which made matters even worse. My experiences over the past ten years had led me to believe that we as professionals had somehow evolved out of that destructive culture of victim blaming and psychological abuse, but this sorry excuse for a clinical director proved otherwise. I confronted her directly, which only resulted in an increase of her abusive behavior. The conditions I was working in were severely triggering to my Post Traumatic Stress Disorder and I began submitting requests for a reasonable accommodation that was guaranteed for individuals with disabilities under the federal Americans with Disabilities Act. Within thirty days, I was fired.

I spent the next year requesting that this agency and the individual who was committing child abuse be held accountable. Everywhere I turned, there were dead-ends and cover-ups. Not surprisingly, there was absolutely no accountability. We are a culture that absolutely despises accountability. Even more disturbing is that we are a culture that not only tolerates sociopathic, psychopathic, and narcissistic behavior, but actually rewards it.

That's a pretty bold statement. You might think, "certainly that must be an exaggeration!" Although, from a clinical perspective, the majority of the population may not meet all of the qualifying criteria for an "official diagnosis," I firmly believe that many of the traits of a clinically diagnosed psychopath, sociopath, or narcissistic personality disorder can be noted as qualities that are encouraged and rewarded in our society. These qualities include complete self-absorption, lack of empathy for the emotions of others, and being disconnected from or devoid of one's own emotions. Nearly anywhere we look in our society, these qualities can be seen, on reality TV shows, from politicians in Washington DC, in the CIA torture program, from law enforcement, in child protective services and related entities, in the behavior of pop stars, and so on. This, in essence, has been the only true trickledown effect that has worked. If this behavior is acceptable at the highest levels of our culture, why would it not saturate all levels? The most obvious area of our culture where lack of compassion and empathy can be seen is the way we treat our most vulnerable populations: the poor, the sick, wounded veterans, single mothers, children, and the elderly.

Many people disagree that we are a "Christian nation," a country that was founded on Christian ethics. The founding fathers were Deists, so yes, they did believe in a God, but they were *adamant* about the separation of church and state, with good reason. There was as much hypocrisy back then, as there is today, around Christian ethics. The prime example of this is the basis of colonialism: arriving on Turtle Island, a land that is already inhabited by Indigenous people that lived their so-called Christian values by ensuring everyone in the society was cared for, especially the children, the elders and the sick. All life was acknowledged as Sacred and respected. The uncharted territories of the tribes were taken by force or through deception and trickery and still continues to this day in many different forms. The United States as a country still have yet to officially recognize the genocide of Indigenous People, 75 million in fact.[16] 75 million Indigenous men, women, and children were brutally murdered or killed by disease. That is the foundation on which our country and the whole of the western hemisphere was built. I have always struggled with seeing any Christian ethics in that.

Most agree that the Holocaust was one of the biggest atrocities in modern history, but what is not widely known is that Adolf Hitler borrowed many tactics from studying the internment camps that were set up for Native Americans as the American territories were being settled. Going even further back, we can see the atrocities committed by Christopher Columbus in the name of land acquisition for Spain – brutal atrocities on peaceful people – and yet we still celebrate the legacy of pain and suffering that this man created every year on Columbus Day. This is the epitome of rewarding psychopathic behavior.

Despite this country's undeniable history of laws based on racism and the genocide, slavery and terrorism that resulted from those racist laws and social norms, media, politicians and a large population in this country insist that the United States is a Christian Nation. If they

---

16   Genocide and American Indian History http://www.americanhistory.oxfordre.com

insist on calling us a Christian nation, there are a lot of amends that we need to make for our history as a Christian country. Each person who claims that they have accepted Christ into their life should take a good honest look at whether or not their behavior and beliefs are aligned with their Christian ideals. After all, their spiritual leader Jesus Christ is responsible for the famous words, "do unto others as you would have done unto me". I was having dinner at some friends' house. They are a model traditional Christian American family, wonderful people whom I absolutely adore. Their eldest son and his family had joined us for dinner. The son began a story of how a homeless man approached him and how he tried to get away from him as quickly as possible, so he didn't have to interact with him. He went on to explain that despite his efforts he was not able to escape an interaction. Through their brief conversation he found out that this homeless man ended up being someone he had attended high school with. I thought that maybe the story would take a turn for the better, that this may have somehow increased the compassion he felt for this man, but that was not the case. He continued on, saying how pathetic this man had become, destroying his life with drugs and alcohol. Attitudes like this are unfortunately not isolated incidents, but rather an epidemic. What people don't seem to understand is that drug addicts and alcoholics are more likely than not using substances to numb pain. Whether it is the pain that a veteran experiences from PTSD after returning from the war, physical pain, the pain of a dysfunctional childhood, the pain of domestic violence, or possibly even pain from a traumatic event that the individual has completely blocked out of their memory. It is certainly not our place to judge an individual as to why they make the decisions that they do. Our one and only obligation is to show them love. That's it.

While passing through New Orleans on the way back from my Mother's funeral, I decided that I wanted to take a chance and venture outside my comfort zone with my photography hobby and take some portrait photos. But rather than taking pictures of people that you might see in magazines, I wanted to capture the unseen, the ones who had been forgotten. One of these was a homeless woman named Shirley. I found her sitting on a park bench in the French Quarter, with a basket containing presumably all her earthly possessions. She was eating luncheon meat that looked like it had already expired. She had on a hospital ID bracelet. She asked me if she could feed a piece of the meat to my dog, but before I could say no, Luna was already swallowing it. So, I sat and talked with Shirley for a while, to hear her story. She had once been a registered nurse, but as could happen to any of us, a slew of tragedies ripped through her life, changing it forever. She had a broken hand and a head injury from being attacked the night before. A couple of weeks before that, her foot had been run over by a car. Without adequate medical insurance, the hospital did the least they could do and released her immediately. She never once asked me for money, but I expressed that I wished I had the financial means to take her for a meal, but I did not. I barely had the money that I needed for gas to get home. Shirley was grateful and content with the spoiled food she had, but she did express that she desperately needed a pair of sunglasses, as she had a medical condition in her eyes that made sunlight excruciatingly painful, so I gave her mine. I asked her to promise me that she would not give up hope, and she did make that promise. We prayed together, I took her photo, and we went our separate ways, both of us having been changed forever by that brief exchange of humanity. As we go about our daily lives with the roofs we have over our heads, with adequate clothing and full bellies, it's comforting to believe that Creator had a plan for those that are poor, downtrodden, and spiritually bankrupt. But the fact is we are Creator's plan for them, and we are failing them miserably. We have become convinced that our material wants are needs, which they are not. More than once in my life, Creator has blessed me with the opportunity to start out from zero and through these experiences I have come to find out that what we need when it comes to material items is very little, and the simpler our diets are, the healthier we are. I have mainly mentioned the Christian perspective of charity and love, but many other faiths hold the same ideals when it comes to these topics and these people of other faiths are just as out of alignment as most American Christians are with their ideals. If they weren't, we would not have the issues that we have on a global level. There is a direct connection between poverty and child sex trafficking, or any type of human trafficking for that matter. Poverty creates the perfect conditions for vulnerable people to be exploited. Poverty leads to desperation and desperate times call for desperate measures, as the saying goes.

A Call to Action

As I HAVE shared with you some of the darkest aspects of my psyche, my life, and the introspection that was required for me to live in accordance with my values in order to transform my life and heal on the deepest levels, I invite each and every one of you to search your own Soul to find what part you play in these plights that are epidemic in our world. No matter what your faith, your beliefs, or your status in life, we can all benefit from taking more accountability for what we contribute to the world. If we believe that Creator, by whatever name you call Source, made us in His/Her image, then it is our responsibility to bring forth that which he/she desires most: Love. We like to believe that we can trust our government, law enforcement, and child protective services to resolve issues such as child sex trafficking, but the sad truth is that individuals in these systems are much more often a part of the problem, whether covertly or overtly, than they are part of a solution. The solution that we so desperately need now is personal accountability, awareness, consciousness, and action.

They say when you keep finding bodies in the river to go up stream and find out what's going on. Time and time again I go up the proverbial stream and at the top I see that it's the toxic male patriarchy that are driving capitalism and colonialism that are causing so much harm to our children, our women, our water, and our Land. They have an insatiable appetite for more and will stop at nothing to get it. So, if this is what is at the core of so many issues worldwide, it would seem the solution would be to bring balance through ReMatriation. That is the very mission of the Rise In Love Foundation, to support individuals, families, communities, and companies in making the shift, creating

Cultures of Safety by healing the collective Mother Wound by brining women together in culture, connection, and conversation. Over the course of my life, I realized that it was my desire to be loved that put me in some of the most compromising situations I have ever found myself in. At one point I started to believe that Love was the problem, but later I realized it was people that had forgotten *how* to Love that are the problem and that Love itself is always the solution.

"Your task is not to seek for love, but merely to seek and find all the barriers within yourself that you have built against it."

- Rumi

Follow Vandee and her work at:
www.risinlovefoundation.org
www.womenofthewhitebuffalo.com

Postscript

As the year 2014 ended, I was just finishing the initial editing process of this book before copywriting and sending the manuscript off to be reviewed by a couple of people I trust. On the afternoon of New Year's Eve, I got a phone call from one of my uncles in Florida. He still associates with some of the people that witnessed what happened to me as a teenager – in fact, one such person is his roommate. When he called to wish me a Happy New Year, at one point in the call he handed his phone off to his roommate, Joni, a woman who frequented the crack houses that I was sold in. She sounded inebriated over the phone and although annoyed with the situation, I did my best to stay compassionate and cordial. She kept going on about how much she looked up to me and what a beautiful woman I had become despite all of the circumstances that I had faced. At one point she said, "I want to remind you how far I have seen you come since I have known you. At one point you were being turned out (trafficked), and now look at all you have." I was overcome with emotion upon her saying that – anger, grief, sadness, and feeling indignant. I wanted to reply sarcastically about her comment about "all that I have," because ironically this year, I lost everything: my career, my home, my community, my ability to work, my Mother, my sense of self-sufficiency. I ended the call as quickly and kindly as I could and went to go sit with all of these emotions and what they meant. First, I realized I had been angered by the fact that her saying this was representative of the fact of how many people knew what had happened to me and did nothing to intervene. Then I realized I was angry that when the proper authorities did intervene, the majority (minus one social worker) held the viewpoint that what I had endured had been my fault. As I continued to unravel this ball of entangled emotion, I decided to once again open my book of daily meditations, and there sat the ultimate answer: we are but earthen vessels created to contain the Sacred Blueprints from Creator. Creator cleared my life of all distractions so that I could complete this book. And once again I felt reassured that He/She was actively working in my life and grateful for even the most painful losses of the past year, because each experience contributed greatly to the writing of this book. And through finishing this book I can offer myself to the world and be of service, by inspiring healing and leading victims on the road to becoming victors.

Special Thanks... I would like to take the opportunity to give a special thanks to the many amazing people that I have been blessed to have in my life. I would like to thank: Jessica Rose for always believing in me no matter what and that time that you bailed me out of jail; Ed Armstrong and his family for showing me what it meant to feel safe and supported; Laurel Rappaport for taking the time to have that life-changing conversation with me, even though you had your doubts, and for being an amazing friend and mentor through the years; Danny Jaramillo for being a shining example of what it is to embody the Bodhisattva/Christ-consciousness; Gurumeet Kaur Khalsa for being the most amazing Kundalini Yoga Teacher and for believing in me when I didn't; Lynn Sanchez for supporting me in healing my Mother Wound and being an incredible professional mentor; Dr. Kartar and Deva Khalsa for supporting my healing by allowing me to do work exchange for continued acupuncture treatments and yoga classes; Dr. Harijot Khalsa for his amazing Shen treatments that brought me immense healing; Gurudarshan Khalsa for her radiant, joyful soul and the beautiful art that she brings to the world; Any and all of the students and clients that I have had the honor to work with, as you have inspired me to keep going; Suhaila and Fran for gently and compassionately keeping me focused on the goal of completing this book; Judson Kusy for being an amazing clinician and for the work he does to combat childhood poverty and trauma. Finally my beautiful and talented friend and editor Karen Erikson Parks, who passed away unexpectedly in June 2018. There are so many more incredible people whom I am forgetting to mention, but I am nonetheless grateful for each and every one of you. Above all I would like to thank Creator, without whom none of this would be possible. And lastly, but certainly not least, I want to thank my Daughter TatankaSkaWin "Tata" SwiftBird, my partner in ReMatriation, for sitting by my side and helping me do the final proofing of this book, and for simply being my beautiful Daughter.